AF599250

TRANSFORMATION, DESIGNED

[ ]EVOLUTION FROM WITHIN

J.J. DE LA TORRE

Ballast Books, LLC
www.ballastbooks.com

Acknowledgment and Disclaimer: To help illustrate the concepts presented, *Transformation, Designed* contains several case studies of successful companies that have effectively leveraged design to transform their offerings and customer experience. The author wishes to acknowledge these companies' contributions to this field while clarifying that all information used was obtained strictly from public sources. Any and all content is purely that of the author. Furthermore, the author makes no representations that the interpretation of the actions and strategies outlined in the book's case studies align with such companies' view.

ISBN: 978-1-964934-02-0

Printed in the Hong Kong

Published by Ballast Books
www.ballastbooks.com

For more information, bulk orders, appearances, or speaking requests, please email: info@ballastbooks.com

To Maria, my life partner and inspiration, and to our incredible children, Cayetano, Borja, and Arantxa, whose curiosity and spirit light up my world. To my family, whose unwavering support and love have always guided me. And to the entire Raven team—thank you for your dedication and drive; together, we are transforming the future by design! This book is for all of you.

CONTENTS

INTRODUCTION

The world is constantly being disrupted by small, fast, lean companies and start-ups. By leveraging technological advancements, these disruptors create unique value propositions that blindside traditional and established players in mainstream markets. Small in size but big in ideas, these start-ups are disrupting traditional companies in industries from banking to airlines and shipping to telecoms.

The challenge for big corporations is how to compete with the lower prices, faster time to market, and superior customer experiences the disruptors have created. What is it that makes the disruptors so successful? What do these companies do differently? How are they building their new value propositions? What is their focus? What are the assets they're creating? How can big corporations react? And what does the way ahead look like?

The answer to all these questions? Design.

It can seem like the almost unimaginably distant past, but in terms of evolutionary history, the emergence of humans' development of tools—and crucially, the use of these implements to change lives and societies—is actually a rather recent occurrence.

It was also a disruptive one. Archaeologists, anthropologists, and biologists all agree that the shift to using tools, the earliest kind of technology, was one of evolution's most drastic, significant, and life-altering milestones.[1] And once they were discovered, there was no turning back.

[1] Kathy D. Schick and Nicholas Toth, Making SIlent Stones Speak (Touchstone, 1994).

From the development of those first prehistoric tools to the industrial revolution and the invention of personal computing, humans haven't stopped innovating, and design has been at the forefront of everything we do. Technological advances have allowed us to explore the outer reaches of space and the depths of the oceans, but it's also impacted the more mundane aspects of our daily lives, and that is the subject of this book.

Our understanding of design has evolved as our expectations and ways of interacting with technology, machines, and tools have moved from being purely functional and practical to a more experiential and engaged approach. In a world where global markets and human experiences are constantly being "transformed" and/or "disrupted" by innovation, the question isn't whether design and transformation are related. The question is: can we embrace design to craft digital transformation and make it successful and meaningful? And if you're reading this book, your specific question is likely: How can I harness the lessons of impactful design to transform my enterprise?

That's what I'm here to tell you. As a recognized global leader in digital transformation who has led more than two hundred digital transformation projects, consulting across a diverse range of industries and organizations, I possess the unique perspective and experience to identify and articulate the specific principles and characteristics of design. This can result in transformative digital experiences, both for a business entity and its varied stakeholders.

In this book, I'll show you how you can use design as a route to digital transformation in your organization. We'll examine the capability of all types of enterprises to adopt the same practices that have made challengers and disruptors successful. You'll see that the road ahead means embracing not only their practices and value propositions but also, perhaps counterintuitively, partnering with those same disruptors. Ultimately, we'll discover that the future will require continuous reinvention and the ability to build unique relationships both inside and outside your enterprise, where partnership and value proposition extension is the norm.

In that vein, I believe that it's possible to look at the countless success stories of digital transformation through emphasis on design, take lessons from them, and then apply those lessons in a way that is relevant to your own enterprise. By laying out these success stories in case study form, I'll break down for you the core concepts of design in the context of digital transformation. Plus, I'll guide you in mapping out your own strategy for an evolutionary leap in practices that will lead you to success.

In addition, in each chapter, you will discover the basic vocabulary and definitions that will provide you with a basis of common language to understand, discuss, plan, develop, and execute a digital transformation powered by design. From defining value proposition, archetypes, and user personas to exploring the use of key methodologies such as design thinking, we will delve into a language that will enable our design-led transformation.

Finally, let me add a note about our current moment. As I write this book, the world is in the throes of responding to COVID-19, a global pandemic forcing sweeping changes upon every industry. This particular pandemic may be contained, but experts assure us that it won't be our only or final disruptor. In fact, disruptors and disasters are constant threats to enterprise health and longevity. At the same time, they present distinct opportunities that can be leveraged if we are attentive, nimble, and responsive to them.

One of the central principles of design for digital transformation is the notion that design is dynamic. It's evolutionary. That means that it can—and must—evolve to respond to the challenges and opportunities of the current moment. It matters less about what the specific challenges and opportunities are and more about whether you've created the design architecture to allow you to pivot toward an effective, efficient response.

So read on! I'm here to help you understand and implement these basic principles to infuse design-led transformation strategies into your organization. Let's begin!

CHAPTER 1

A NEW BEGINNING

"The great growling engine of change—technology."

—Alvin Toffler

We live in an era of change fueled by technological advances, democratization of information, changing customer expectations, and a lowering of regulatory barriers.

A critical factor in adapting to these changes is embedding concepts such as design, experience, and customer experience into your company strategy.

In this chapter, we'll identify the emerging trends that are not only shaping the markets but also influencing how companies evolve. Plus, we'll develop a deeper understanding of the concept of digital transformation. But first, let's start with a quick overview of how we got here.

Nineteen ninety was a banner year.

While it was preceded by a number of developments that led to the internet as we know it today, 1990 was the year when British engineer and scientist Tim Berners-Lee invented the World Wide Web. Thirty years later, Berners-Lee reflected on his role in the launch of a hyper-connected world, a collective "public square" where many problems are being solved—or could be. While he noted the profound power of global connectivity and many of the benefits it had conferred upon people around the world, he also pointed out that the internet's development was not—could not be—static.

"Given how much the web has changed in the past thirty years," he remarked, "it would be defeatist and unimaginative to assume that the web as we know it can't be changed for the better in the next thirty. If we give up on building a better web now, then the web will not have failed us. We will have failed the web."[2]

The "web," of course, is no longer just available on big, clunky machines that sit on our desks. As its very name suggests, its filaments extend into nearly every area of our lives, across a range of devices, large and small, fixed and mobile. And if you take five minutes—a great thought exercise—to do a quick brainstorm, you'll likely be surprised by just how much Berners-Lee's invention has taken over your life and your business.

Of course, in the three decades since Berners-Lee flipped the "ON" switch on the World Wide Web, numerous other

[2] "30 years on, what's next for #TheWeb?" Web Foundation, March 12, 2019, https://webfoundation.org/2019/03/web-birthday-30/.

actors—inventors, engineers, entrepreneurs, and hobbyist dabblers—have all made their mark on our shared digital space. Collectively, those who have moved the needle are often referred to as **disruptors**, folks who challenge the status quo and invite us all to dream more imaginatively about how digital tools can be used, whether for commerce or some greater good—or both. The emergence of mobile devices—smartphones, specifically—has pushed these disruptors to further redefine the boundaries of human creativity and ingenuity, introducing goods and services for even the most basic things that we now consider absolutely essential to our daily lives.

Embracing Digital Technologies

Before we get too far, let's make sure we're on the same page regarding key definitions. It is quite common to confuse digitization with digitalization, digitalization with digital transformation, or digital transformation with digital disruption. However, it's important to have an accurate understanding of each concept to ensure you're applying them effectively within your organization. With that in mind, let's take a moment to look at what we mean by each of these terms:

- **Digitization** is the simplest form of using technology to improve a process or an experience. It's where you take something that is physical and digitize it into a system.

  For example, a paper form to open a bank account is filled in by the customer and handed in to their branch. The bank clerk then digitizes it by manually inputting it into the bank's computer system.

- **Digitalization** is when you take manual processes and add a digital element to make it more efficient without changing anything in the experience or creating competitive value. For example, the form for opening a bank account is now completed and submitted online.

The main driver for digitalization is to improve the efficiency of the process. You haven't actually changed the process or experience. The new customer still needs to fill in a new account form. It's just that now they fill it in online rather than on paper. This means the bank can now deal with more account applications than they did previously because they no longer need to be individually entered into the computer system by the bank clerk.

Digitalization is a great way to improve and measure efficiency. What it doesn't do is improve or measure your customer experience. How did your customer experience the journey, product, process, or interaction with your business?

A lot of companies focus on digitalization thinking that it's also transformation. It's not. Most companies mistake digitalizing processes with transforming their business, but in reality, they're still using their traditional business model with the same channels, same media, and same behavior base. Businesses can spend a lot of time and money digitalizing their operation without seeing a corresponding increase in customer satisfaction and experience.

- **Digital transformation**—the focus of this book—is a way to improve and evolve your entire business model based on creating a new experience with your customers powered by data and implication technology. It's not a project; it's a paradigm shift. You're changing how you capture value and what the value proposition is for the end user. It's transforming the experience beyond the product or service. It means identifying and understanding your most valuable assets and creating new experiences based on data and enabled by digital technologies.

- **Digital disruption**[3] is about business revolution. It implies a new experience, a new business model, and a new business platform outside of your core business, which will reinterpret your assets.

As you can see, each of these key terms are related but distinct! Understanding the terminology and knowing when and how to use each concept is crucial for transforming your business through design.

Digitalize	Transformation
→ Focus on Efficiency → Focus on Process → Customer as a Result → Same Business Model	→ Business Model Evolution → New User & Collaborator Experience → Operate as a Platform
Take manual processes and add a digital element to make them more efficient without changing anything in the experience or creating a new competitive value.	Understand which is your most valuable asset, analyze it, and create new experiences that adapt to the main wishes and needs of the people in the actual context. This is a constant process of value creation.

Emerging Trends—It's a New World!

The mass availability of smartphones was like the activation of a "reset" button. Everything that consumers and even business owners knew about commerce shifted. Suddenly, both business owners and consumers were available to reach each other 24/7. The very notion of "convenience" began to be redefined . . . and quickly.

New forms of delivering goods, fresh means of providing services, and novel ways of paying for them—all of these

[3] See *Disruption, Designed,* the second book in the series, to learn more.

variables began to shape the contours of a brand-new ecosystem, one in which everyone's expectations were reshaped. Design—intentional, strategic design—was clearly going to play a vital, central role. The world shifted from a resource-based economy to a data- and actionable-insights-based one, with start-ups emerging across the globe and employing a laser focus on creating new experiences for the customer.

Design is now being embraced as the ultimate enabler to devise, set in motion, and deliver to customers a compelling value proposition. We find ourselves in a world where innovation is no longer an activity that requires millions of dollars and years in development. In fact, it's exactly the opposite!

With the commoditization of technology and technological services, we're moving from a problem-based approach to a solution-based model focusing on experience engagement. New solutions are emerging with a value proposition focused on the end user and their interaction with the solution itself.

In the last ten years alone, advances in technology have accelerated, enabling solutions that were not previously thought possible. Nowadays, it's faster, easier, and cheaper than ever before to develop and deploy technological solutions that can reach millions of customers in seconds. Agile methodologies have enabled fast turnaround and updates of platforms and solutions, while consumer-focused digital companies have created a new focus on design and user experience that has become a key component in the adoption of any value proposition.

Technology is not only used to capture information but also to create an ecosystem of elements that share a common layer of information—in other words, to sync things. Your coffee machine is synced to your air conditioning, which is synced to your music, and everything is synced to your app. So when we talk about an ecosystem, what we see is new technological forces being used not in isolation but to build experiences, create visuals, and produce a new value proposition that is truly 100 percent multichannel or, ideally, omnichannel.

What is omnichannel? It is a multichannel approach to sales that focuses on providing a seamless customer experience, whether the client is shopping on a mobile device or on a laptop or in a brick-and-mortar store. Many customers will go online to research a product before going into the store, while others will go online to continue their research once in store. In each instance, their experience should be exactly the same.

Without multichannel, there can be no omnichannel, but where omnichannel excels is that it connects all the channels by creating a single user experience. Your customer has the same experience in whichever place they choose to engage with you. In essence, omnichannel businesses focus on the entire customer experience, not the individual experiences on different channels.

Research has shown that businesses with strong omnichannel customer engagement retain an average of 89 percent of their customers compared to 33 percent of those with weak or no omnichannel customer engagement. Those numbers certainly speak for themselves!

Amazon is a great example of omnichannel commerce in action. What started out as an online-only business has transformed into a truly omnichannel experience. Not only can customers access their profile via the Amazon website, but they can also access this same information on their mobile app, Alexa device, smartwatch, or in a store. In addition, while customers can place and track their orders online, they can also choose to collect in-store or at various locker locations. Or they can have it delivered to their door!

We Are in a Movement!

We are moving away from focusing on transactions and competing to attract and close a sale on the spot by converting target customers into actual customers. Instead, we are becoming a world where we compete for attention. As such, we now focus on audiences, where we aim to establish connections, generate trust, and then capitalize on that relationship.

This is a profound change. It turns a conversion game, focused on the number of adverts that are trying to close a transaction, into a desire to build an audience by generating a community and a sense of belonging.

Legoland is a good example of this. Your experience on the day you visit is important, but so too is the preparation, the buildup to the day, the excitement before you arrive, and how you capitalize on that. How do you keep the theme park at the forefront of the consumers' consciousness, build on the memories created, and encourage them to look forward to creating new ones on their next visit?

Legoland's core philosophy is to be more than just a theme park. It is a place to learn while having fun, spend quality time with family, and increase creativity and imagination. This creates an emotional attachment for many parents, leading them to choose Legoland as their attraction of choice in order to develop their children's cognitive, emotional, and behavioral skills—all in an environment in which they can participate and derive as much enjoyment as their children. Getting involved, socializing while having fun, and taking pleasure from the experience become important motivations.

It's also what drives their online engagement through a community of bloggers. These bloggers refer to the valuable experience they have in the centers and express not only their recommendations and suggestions to potential visitors but also what they intend to do on their next visit. They are already planning to go back. Legoland has leveraged "experience" as a critical driver of online consumer engagement both in terms of raising the level of relational exchange as well as in fostering emotional bonds to their centers. This is a valuable resource of user-generated advocacy and publicity, which helps to build an audience.

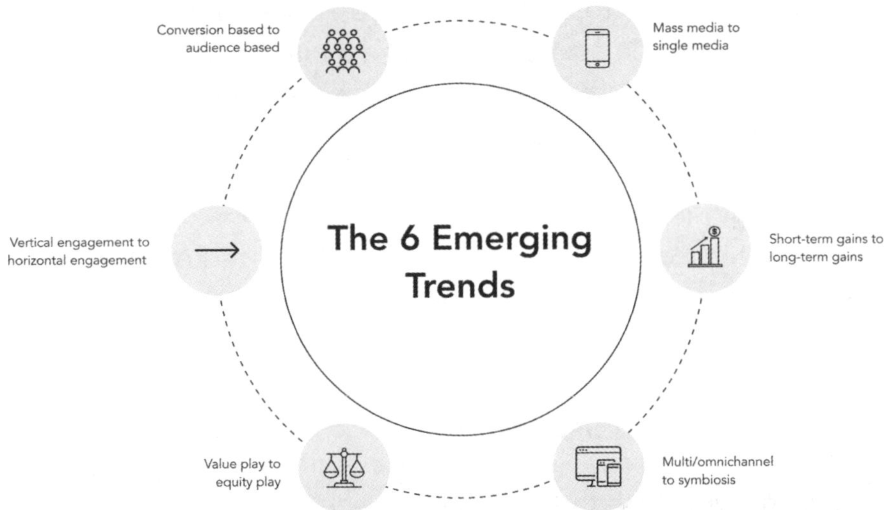

This movement from **conversion based to audience based** is the first of six emerging trends in the new ecosystem.

It changes the way you take a product or service to market. First, you need to plant the seed, generate the need, and establish a connection with the audience. Then, once the customer buys or consumes your product or service, you need to ensure that this is part of an ongoing overall experience of engaging with your company and establishing a continuing relationship with that customer. This is particularly important as consumers become increasingly empowered (via regulation) to opt in or out of marketing messaging.

The second emerging trend is the move from **mass media to single media**.

The traditional view of marketing a product or service is to use mass media—newspapers, radio, TV, social media—in a blanket approach to broadcast your message to everyone and hope that it hits someone who is interested. Through technology, we have better access to data and the ability to broadcast a tailored message to a more targeted audience. Internet media is so cheap that the cost of producing a number of tailored messages for different target audiences—based on demographics, age groups, ethnicity, and so on—is not prohibitive.

We saw the use of this type of targeted messaging in the US presidential election. The Donald Trump campaign used social media to send out tailored messages to targeted groups of voters in an attempt to influence the way they cast their votes.

This leads nicely to the third emerging trend, which involves utilizing the customer information you hold to move from **vertical to horizontal engagement**.

It requires companies to change from a vertical approach, where you work with the customer up and down the supply chain, to a horizontal approach, where you create a platform business. Conversely, the horizontal approach involves moving from a transactional relationship with the customer to leveraging your assets (the data you hold on them—their likes, preferences, and needs) and collaborating with others within a wider related market.

For instance, say a barbecue manufacturing company leverages its customer database to build a customer profile and allow targeted messaging to offer a subscription box containing BBQ meat. Building on this, the company might start to offer sauces or tools and equipment, then drinks or marinades and perhaps even outdoor living products/services or experiences.

Taking this broader view of your business encompasses the fourth emerging trend of moving from **short-term gains to long-term gains**. This is the difference between the purchase economy of one-off transactions and the lease or service economy where you have a pay-as-you-go component.

For instance, instead of buying their car outright, a customer might lease it and pay by the mileage. In other words, they pay as they consume. Then, when a new car model comes out or their needs change, they have the opportunity to quickly and easily upgrade.

This moves the relationship with your customer from a short-term, one-off transactional one to a longer-term engagement allowing you to match their evolving needs. Perhaps they have just started a family and need a bigger car. Or their employer changed to a hybrid or remote work model post-COVID, so they are now working mainly from home and don't want to pay the full price for a car that is just sitting in their driveway. Whatever their unique situation, you can meet their needs, even as they change over time.

The fifth emerging trend is the shift from **value play to equity play**.

As a business, if your focus is on value play, then you are measuring the value of your business based on immediate transaction value, income, and revenue. This means you need to sell and sell and keep on selling.

When you move to equity play, you begin focusing on building your audience. Of course, you may end up selling much less. But that's not necessarily as bad as it seems at first glance.

Let's say you have a customer base of ten million, but only two hundred of these customers are actually purchasing your product or service. On its face, that doesn't seem like a lot, but you're still getting data from the whole database, and this is an extremely valuable asset. The value of your company is now not only linked to its P&L (the direct profit and loss value) but also to the future value that you might derive from your data and the monetization opportunities it provides.

Consider the value of WhatsApp and Instagram, both bought for millions of dollars and completely unrelated to their actual value in terms of revenue. Their value is in building audiences and creating experiences for those audiences. They have millions of potential consumers that they interact with on a regular, if not daily, basis, and the data capture that goes with that is, in many ways, priceless.

The final emerging trend is the move from **multichannel or omnichannel to symbiosis**.

As you already learned, multichannel involves having different ways or "channels" through which to talk to your customer. Prior to the internet, this might have been by phone or in a store.

From 2010 onward, as the internet evolved, the concept of omnichannel was introduced. Many companies spent millions of dollars to ensure continuity across all their channels. However, a customer who goes into the store wants a very different experience from one who prefers to use the website. This is again different from someone (perhaps a millennial!) who wants to do everything via the app.

Symbiosis is the evolution of the omnichannel idea. It involves designing meaningful interactions for each type of customer requirement.

Take banking, for example. Say I want to be able to do a bank transfer at any time using the app. However, if I'm thinking about taking out a loan or applying for a mortgage, I want to go into a branch, sit down with an adviser, take my time, and actually talk about the various options with an expert. So the symbiosis approach is about having different interactions with customers to ensure they get the right experience to meet their individual needs.

In reality, what this new movement with its emerging trends means for businesses is that we need to evolve the value proposition into an experience-driven proposition.

Evolving the Value Proposition

A value proposition is all about perceived value. It identifies the benefits (both tangible and intangible) that a customer can expect when buying or interacting with a product or service. It has an intrinsic value that is perceived by the customer. When done well, it inspires a customer's belief in that product or service, acts as a competitive differentiator, and motivates potential customers to choose one product or service over another. When the perceived value is higher than the actual value (cost), then you create a relationship with the customer rather than simply having a business transaction.

A value proposition is your chance to tell your target market why they should do business with you. What makes you better than everyone else? How do you do it uniquely well? How does this add value to your customers' lives? A great value proposition can be the difference between whether a customer explores deeper into your website or hits the back button.

In order to create a compelling value proposition, you need to thoroughly understand your target market's needs, wants, and problems and how your product or service can meet or solve them. This is one of the areas in which technology-based startups do exceptionally well. They develop fictional characters that represent their intended target customer, which allows them to create new solutions for existing problems and a compelling value proposition focused solely on their identified end user.

A great value proposition example is Grammarly:

- It's simple to understand what's being offered: **Great Writing, Simplified.**
- It identifies what needs/wants/problems it's meeting/solving: **Compose bold, clear, mistake-free writing.**
- It establishes how it is uniquely placed to do that: **AI-powered writing assistant that picks up mistakes in grammar, spelling, and formatting and suggests improvements/corrections.**
- The addition of a video on the landing page means you are immediately drawn into how it works and the benefit it provides.

Your value proposition must provide the customer with a clear understanding of what you do, who you do it for, and how you do it differently. Long gone are the times of creating standard, robust, feature-rich, and expensive solutions where the average user utilizes less than 10 percent of the available features.

Just to illustrate this point, consider Microsoft Excel. There are hundreds of features and functions in Excel that are not used by the vast majority of users. That's not to say they are never used. Every single one of those functions or features was the result of customer requests. Remember, when a product like Excel is being built, it's aiming to be used by hundreds of millions of people for millions of different applications. To keep big customers happy, features that are unique to their business but of little value to others may be added. Specialist users like mathematicians, data scientists, or statisticians may use some functions that the other one hundred million users are unaware even exist. Even if only one in one thousand people is interested in that feature, it still means over one hundred thousand people in the world use it.

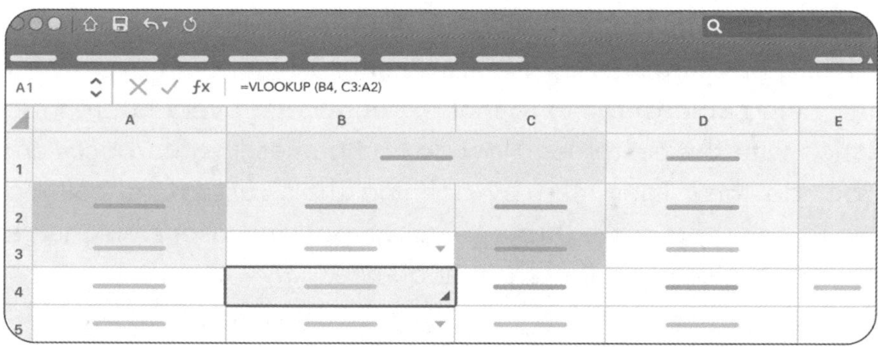

Today, the customer is at the center of the experience, and the solution must meet the exact needs of that user. Simplicity is the key, and, from a usability perspective, less is more. Cost and return on investment (ROI) will continue to be key considerations, but as development budgets move from the IT department to marketing, and with digital presence at the core of the brand and sales channel, it's paramount that, through design, the overall customer experience is foundational to your product development.

Starbucks is an example of this fundamental shift in approach. They reinvented the functional and undifferentiated action of drinking coffee as an experience where coffee became part of the overall brand value proposition. In reality, we don't go to Starbucks just for great coffee but rather for the enjoyable experience. From entry to exit, at every touchpoint—reaching the counter, choosing and customizing our coffee, selecting a sandwich or cake, enjoying the atmosphere, and catching up with emails at one of the workspaces—this person-centric approach is what converts customers to brand advocates.

Uber also crafted an experience that simplified the process of getting around a city. The complexity of the system is completely hidden and irrelevant. The customer experience is the priority, and this simplicity is the key to its success.

Both these examples demonstrate where design goes beyond basic aesthetics. It's about encapsulating an experience and being able to recreate that experience at every future interaction with the customer. How do companies like Starbucks and Uber do this? They start by defining their customers, collaborators, and end users through archetypes and user personas to better understand their target audience.

Defining Your Target Audience and Customers

Customers/clients

Collaborators

End users

Understanding your target audience starts with defining who that audience is:

- **Customers/clients:** the people consuming or interacting with your goods/services or value proposition
- **Collaborators:** your employees. By thinking of them as collaborators in your business, it puts them on equal footing with customers to the extent that you need to understand and focus on both to achieve your value proposition.
- **End users:** the person who is consuming your value proposition. Both customers and collaborators can be end users.

These entities are then defined by leveraging the archetype creation methodology, which allows the development of a fictional character that encompasses the experience drivers, behavioral triggers, and key characteristics of these groups. This archetype method is used to create new value propositions.

The customer archetype is a description or narrative about the personality type or role of your ideal customer. It generally focuses on their behavior and relationship with your product. What do they want? What do they lack? What are they looking for in their interaction with your product now and in the future? Developing a customer archetype allows you to predict their behavior, their needs, and their concerns and then use that knowledge as a competitive advantage to satisfy them. More importantly, it allows you to understand the emotional factor, and connecting with the emotions of your user is the key to transformation. What role is your target customer trying to fulfill by using your product or service? What is their motivation?

An early example of an archetype used in marketing is the "early adopter." This usually describes a type of customer who uses a new product, innovation, or technology before anyone else. They are likely to be risk takers who will happily pay more for the product or service in order to be considered "ahead of the game," at the "forefront of innovation," or "in at the start," thereby raising their social or business status.

Next, a user persona involves creating a character, a fictional person, who is an example of your ideal type of customer. To do this, you might consider their attitudes, values, perceptions, beliefs, habits, and interests as well as create a personal profile:

- Name
- Gender
- Age
- Income
- Education level

- Marital status
- Children
- Occupation
- Hobbies
- Where they live (suburban, rural, urban)

Javier García

52 · Bachelor's · London
Single · Non-Binary · CEO

Personality

Introvert — Extrovert
Thinking — Feeling
Judging — Prospecting
Assertive — Turbulent
Intuitive — Observant

Attitudes

Javier is proactive about financial planning and believes in the importance of preparing for retirement. They are cautious and prefer to have a well-structured plan for their future.

Values

Family, financial security, stability, and growth.

Perceptions

Skeptical about government pension schemes due to regulatory uncertainties and a declining replacement rate. Believes private savings are essential for a comfortable retirement.

Skills

Software
E-commerce
Leadership

Motivations

- Ensuring a comfortable and secure retirement.
- Maximizing investment returns while minimizing risks.
- Leveraging tax benefits to enhance savings.
- Providing financial support for their children's education and futures.

Goals

- Increase retirement savings by 20% over the next five years.
- Find investment products offering both security and growth potential.
- Diversify investment portfolio to mitigate risks.
- Achieve financial independence before the age of 60.

Pain Points

- High uncertainty in the regulatory environment affecting pension schemes.
- Low interest rates on traditional savings accounts.
- Limited access to personalized financial advice aligning with their goals.
- Difficulty finding reliable and user-friendly digital investment platforms.

Laura Sánchez

28 · Master's · London
Single · Non-Binary · Digital Manager

Personality

Introvert — Extrovert
Thinking — Feeling
Judging — Prospecting
Assertive — Turbulent
Intuitive — Observant

Attitudes

Laura is tech-savvy and values convenience and innovation. They are open to new financial products and prefer digital solutions.

Values

Innovation, growth, financial independence, and long-term planning.

Perceptions

Believes traditional banking and investment solutions are outdated. Prefers platforms offering a seamless and engaging user experience.

Skills

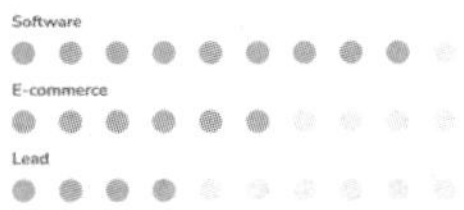

Motivations

- Achieving financial independence and security.
- Learning more about investment opportunities and growing wealth.
- Using technology to streamline and simplify financial management.
- Building a solid financial foundation for future life goals, such as buying a home or starting a business.

Goals

- Save 20% of their income annually for long-term goals.
- Explore and invest in digital financial solutions and platforms.
- Create a diverse investment portfolio that includes stocks, bonds, and other assets.
- Increase financial literacy and confidence in managing investments.

Pain Points

- Overwhelmed by the plethora of investment options and platforms.
- Difficulty finding trustworthy and transparent financial advice.
- Limited understanding of complex financial products and their benefits.
- Concerns about the security of online financial transactions and data privacy.

In essence, you are aiming to discover: Who is this customer? What is their goal? And what is stopping them from achieving their goal? This will help you grow and improve your business by uncovering different ways people search for, buy, and use products/services, allowing you to focus your efforts on improving the experience for real people in real situations.

One of the most important aspects of creating both archetypes and personas is that they must be based on actual data insights. You shouldn't simply construct stereotypical users. These insights can be gathered through many avenues, including:

- User interviews
- Observation of data from actual users
- Customer support logs
- Web analytics
- Analyzing research findings to identify patterns
- Talking to your collaborators who are dealing directly with customers

Using the archetype creation methodology transforms the way organizations think about their customers and drives the shift from traditional value propositions to experience-driven propositions.

The Move to Experience-Driven Propositions

The new world requires a shift away from the traditional value chains, where companies are very clear about what they are doing in terms of their scope of operation, to something more like an ecosystem. Banks are no longer providing loans; they're outsourcing the knowledge or reselling the loans to other companies. More and more airlines are outsourcing some of their core capabilities to other companies while they focus on engagement. Telecom providers are partnering with other companies in the ecosystem to actually build a proposition rather than trying to create everything themselves. This change is supported by a younger generation fully conversant with technology as well as new ways of operating and consuming products and services.

Traditionally, if you were a big corporation, you would be competing with another big corporation in your industry—big bank versus big bank, big insurance company versus big insurance company, big name versus big name. Today, whatever your industry, you could be competing with three guys in their garage basically aggregating businesses to provide the customer with what they want. Ultimately, the big companies may become obsolete. It's happening already in the insurance and telecom industries.

Consider Uber, the largest transportation company in the world—yet they don't own any vehicles. Facebook/Meta, the biggest media company in the world, is not actually creating anything. The only content Facebook creates is what Mark Zuckerberg posts or likes. Alibaba has no inventory but is the largest and most valuable retailer. Airbnb has no real estate, yet it is bigger than the largest hotel chain. And Skype has almost no infrastructure.

All these companies have been called one of two things: format invaders or infrastructure parasites. Effectively, what they do is take your business and create an experience-driven proposition that is much simpler, easier to understand, and direct to the end user. This is not about the number or breadth of products that corporations tend to focus on. These guys concentrate on a single thing, and they lever this single thing to perfection. Once they've done that, they speed off and create something new and focus solely on that.

For example, under the traditional model, as you might find with a bank, you make the products, take them to market, service those products, and then support them with your infrastructure. However, a format invader will focus on a single element of the value chain—for instance, loans. They support the customer throughout the whole experience, perhaps offering new payment methods like Apple Pay or Amazon Pay, and find new ways to reach and engage with the end user.

Digital Upheavals Quicken the Eventuality of Disruption

Disruption Driven by Digital Advancement

TYPE 1: Service Displacement
Disruption resulting from new innovations, rendering incumbent solutions irrelevant

TYPE 2: Infrastructure Parasite
Products leveraging competitors' infrastructures, ultimately delivering their hosts' value with viral momentum

Instagram
facebook

TYPE 3: Dominant Design
Products setting the trends on user experience and dominating with the power of design

Obviously, technology is the great enabler of this type of digital transformation. In fact, technology combined with strategy, leadership, and culture drives business transformation and innovation. However, some companies are making better use of technology than others.

The biggest gap is between the disruptors (Facebook, Uber, Airbnb) and the traditional companies (banks, telecoms, insurance brokers, government). Both have the same exposure to technology, both have the ability to create the same type of products and services, but one is outperforming the other when it comes to focusing on the overall experience. How do they do this? By collecting data and generating insights.

Data and Insights

Without any doubt, one of the key elements shaping digital transformation is the use of data and the creation of real-time customer insights. From basic performance and usage analytics to advanced predictive dynamic models evolved machine learning and then artificial intelligence (AI), a branch of computer science focused on creating systems that mimic human intelligence behavior and allow them to perform complex tasks autonomously. Data will become the driving force to "consume" or "live" experiences and therefore transform companies. Organizations that embrace data will be able to not only anticipate demand and customer needs but also streamline their operations, value chains, and value propositions and even improve employee retention. The usage of data will become a clear differentiator for any enterprise or company, and how data is used to shape experiences will become the enabler of future business growth.

Most companies have more data than they know what to do with, and they often underestimate its value. The challenge is to leverage the data you have while creating new opportunities for data streams in the future. This is the hallmark of high-performing businesses. By increasing the data that can be effectively used, companies also increase their analytics capability. This provides the insight required to make better decisions based on how they're operating and what the customer is doing.

In time, predictive analytics, machine learning, and deep learning will be critical to automation. To clarify, **predictive analytics** involves the use of statistics and data models for the construction of future scenarios based on historical data or similar inputs. An example of this is the prediction of product or service demand or consumer behavior. **Machine learning** is a subset of artificial intelligence techniques focused on building models and algorithms that are capable of learning from data, improving their decisions or outputs over time based on a larger amount of data. And **deep learning** is a field of machine learning based on artificial neural networks that mimics the human learning process for data analysis. It is used in voice and image recognition, among other things. By automating interaction in low-value tasks, you free up your collaborators to focus on tasks that create the most value from their skills.

To fully embed data and analytics, including AI, into the development of customer experiences, integration will be the key that leads to automation. As such, we need to consider that the traditional approach to integration tends to rely on application programming technology (APIs), which are resource intensive in terms of cost and time. However, we will be looking to apply data and analytics in a more flexible manner, which will require rapid integration solutions that extend the reach of technology across a wider range of processes, effectively improving the customer experience.

Experiences Change Expectations

"The technology you use impresses no one.
The experience you create with it is everything."

—Sean Gerety

Customers' expectations are fluid. Why fluid? Because you can't hold or grab a fluid; it moves and evolves naturally. Your customers' expectations behave in exactly the same way.

Today, we can certainly say that the last best experience your customer has becomes the minimum expectation that they will have anywhere. This simple statement has a profound impact on how consumers view the companies they deal with. It also highlights why companies need to focus on their customers in order to build appropriate experience-driven propositions.

Imagine, for instance, that it's the first time you're boarding a plane with Wi-Fi. As soon as you fasten your safety belt, you notice a sign that says "Wi-Fi Available." Remember, it's the first time that you are experiencing this on a plane. As a result, you're curious, so you ask about it and continue searching until you get yourself online. You're thrilled! Now connected to the internet at twenty thousand feet, you take a selfie, get on Skype, and even pay your bills.

You'll enjoy this moment, and without even noticing you're doing it, you'll also be setting a new expectation for your next flight. The next time you board a plane, you'll expect Wi-Fi to be widely available, independent of the airline or route you are taking. We now have a minimum customer expectation defined for the flying industry as a whole, not just the individual airlines.

This is what happened when Emirates airlines started offering internet connection during their flights. Their customers' expectations changed forever. Now, no matter who they are flying with or where they are flying to, they expect to have access to Wi-Fi.

Once a customer has discovered it, it becomes a hygiene factor. A hygiene factor, also called a dissatisfier, is a feature of a product or service that is expected and will make a customer unhappy (or dissatisfied) if it doesn't exist. In this example, Wi-Fi has become a hygiene factor.

Now, let's imagine you just took an Uber. You're not an avid user of this service, but you've been using it sporadically for a while. You've never had a problem with the app or a driver. However, this time, your Uber driver took the wrong route and did so without even consulting you. As a result, your trip took much longer and might have even been more costly than expected. Now, you, as an Uber customer, are not satisfied with the service and give a feedback rating of one star for the trip. Immediately, Uber asks you for more information and opens a case. In a matter of minutes, they have refunded you the cost of the trip with an apology on behalf of the driver.

Receiving this type of interaction and refund is unexpected because you didn't know that your feedback would be acted on immediately by the system. Furthermore, this is the first time that you've complained about anything and gotten a case solved in minutes without human intervention. Now, as it happened in the previous example, your expectations about customer care and complaint management have been redefined, and a minimum expectation about how complaints should be handled by any company you deal with has been created.

Evolved Customer Experience Expectations

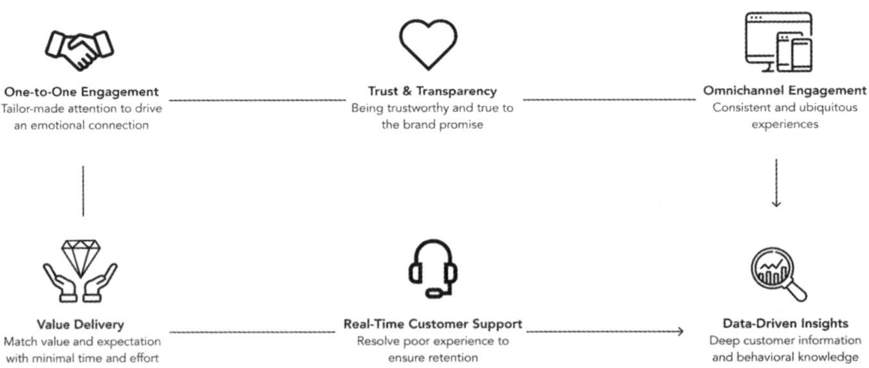

While the two examples have in common the ability to redefine a minimum expectation, they are quite different in nature. The first one changes the customer expectation within the same industry—airlines/flights. On the other hand, the second changes the customer's expectation of the complaint management process in any company, in any industry that they come into contact with.

That minimum expectation is always redefined. It doesn't matter how good you are today because your competitors will match that. What matters is how good you are tomorrow—how you keep evolving.

That always-evolving mentality is not something that generally exists in a traditional company. The mindset in these companies tends to be a perfected product mindset. Perfect the product, perfect the pricing, perfect the distribution, perfect the sales channel, perfect how to market it and how to ship it. But they fail to consider that what seems "perfect" today won't seem so perfect tomorrow once innovative competitors have raised the bar higher.

Evolving Mindset

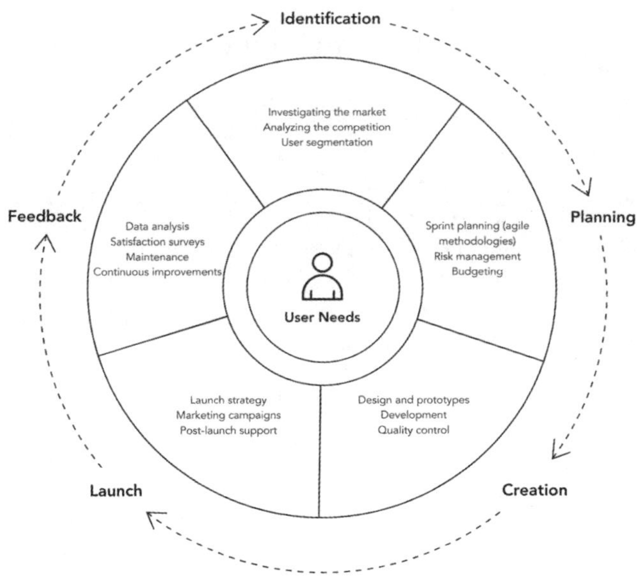

As products and companies become more connected, incumbents are increasingly exposed to these types of experience redefinition dilemmas. However, the second example is the one that should concern companies the most, as it forces them to compete in terms of customer experience irrespective of their domain, category, or industry. From a customer perspective, a telecom incumbent will be compared with the latest fintech start-up regarding their experience and across any process that the customer engages with. From onboarding to customer management, the expectation will be permanently redefined based on the best last experience.

That is why we call this phenomenon **fluid expectations**—to reflect the fact that these experiences and subsequent expectations are transferred between industries and processes. The key implication of this fluid expectation phenomenon is that it forces us to compete on experience rather than one product or service competing against another. This is where companies must start their digital transformation.

Linear Process of the Perfected Product Mindset

The customer no longer wants the cheapest or the fastest. They want an experience. Seventy-five percent of low-income customers are willing to pay up to 30 percent extra for an experience. Eighty-five percent of customers, in particular millennials, expect the mobile version to outperform the desktop version of a company's digital presence. From an end user perspective, you have a customer that is much better informed and who has many more choices than before.

Switching is also easier. Around 80 percent of customers said they would switch suppliers or providers if it was easier, and the surveys suggest, now that it is easier to switch, that's exactly what they will do!

Digital technology has created new rules of customer engagement, from how customers interact with a company to how they pay for services. Unsurprisingly, this affects the loyalty customers feel toward a business and the likelihood of them switching.

The main changes driven by new digital technology are in three fundamental components of the customer experience:

- **Promotion and selling:** word of mouth and peer reviews are used to promote products and services rather than traditional marketing techniques.
- **Enabling transactions:** at the time of the transaction, payment information is kept and stored using lean yet robust technologies, a step up from the complex, multi-layered traditional payment systems that frustrate returning consumers.
- **Supporting customers:** there's a reliance on self-support or pure digital support in contrast to the large infrastructures of people used by traditional enterprises to support their customers across all the various channels.

At this point, you may read the bullets above and think, *Yes, we're doing all that*. But digital transformation is not just about putting in place processes using digital technology. It needs to be a designed experience.

In 1966, in a memo to all employees, Thomas J. Watson Jr. carved out a single definition of design: "Good design is good business." Today, in the post-pandemic world, good design is not only about steering a good business; it's imperative for business survival. The ability to adapt quickly to supply chain disruptions, time to market pressures, and rapidly changing customer expectations through designed digital transformation is critical. This realization is highlighted by the International Data Corporation Worldwide Digital Transformation Spending Guide (May 2020), which forecasts that spending on digital transformation technologies and services will grow 10.4 percent to 1.3 trillion dollars in contrast to dramatic reductions in overall technology spending.

The first step for companies looking to transform digitally is to define their customers' needs and build that into the value proposition from which the business and product design can be derived. Thus, the value proposition will be encapsulated through a designed experience. This not only impacts how things operate but also the underlying processes that enable a particular experience. The business will need to reevaluate these processes as well as their capabilities and enabling technologies. In essence, the organization will need to evolve.

Digital Transformation Changes Businesses

"Technological change is not additive; it is ecological. A new technology does not merely add something; it changes everything."

—Neil Postman

Digital transformation begins and ends with how you think about and engage with customers. Simply put, it means taking a customer-centric approach.

Most companies already talk about putting the customer first, but advances in digital technology are forcing them to make good on this promise, particularly with companies like Apple and Amazon setting new expectations around user experience both online and offline. Customers expect businesses to respond quickly to inquiries, to customize products and services, and to provide easy access to the information they need when they need it.

Customer centricity extends far beyond marketing and product design to become a cultural element underpinning all core decisions across all areas of the business. Committing fully to digital transformation fundamentally changes the way a company operates and delivers value to customers through the integration of technology into all aspects of the business. It requires a cultural change with organizations prepared to challenge the "business as usual" mentality, experiment, and get comfortable with failure. In some cases, it can mean walking away from long-standing business practices and processes.

	Digitalization	**Transformation**
Definition	Conversion of analog processes and documents to digital	Integral change involving culture, models, and technology
Focus	Technical and efficient	Strategic and customer centric
Objective	Improve existing processes	Fundamentally change how the organization operates
Impact	Limited to certain areas	Spans the entire organization
Example	Digitize paper records into databases	Create new business models based on digital technologies

Netflix is a great example of this. It started out as a mail order service competing with brick-and-mortar rental stores. Through digital transformation, using advances in wide-scale streaming technology, it now competes with traditional broadcast and cable TV networks and production studios by offering a huge variety of on-demand content at competitive prices.

Now, not only does Netflix have the ability to stream video content directly to customers, but it has also gained unprecedented insight into their viewing habits and preferences. This data is used to inform all aspects of the business from the design of its user experience to the development of new shows and movies. This also leads to a content recommendation system driven by artificial intelligence.

At this point, it's worth reiterating that digital transformation is not just about technology. According to a *Harvard Business Review* article in 2019, 70 percent of all digital transformation initiatives do not reach their goals, resulting in nine hundred billion dollars of investment going to waste. Why? Because while digital technologies have the potential to provide efficiency gains and greater customer intimacy, if organizations lack the right mindset, and their current business practices and processes are flawed, then digital transformation will simply magnify those flaws. Common pitfalls include:

- Deciding your business just needs a new digital technology tool, such as a new app, payment option, or customer complaint system, rather than a complete strategic rethink.
- Purchasing a one-size-fits-all, off-the-shelf digital transformation solution rather than tailoring the digital transformation solution needed for your individual business.

- Thinking you already know the answer to what your customer wants from you now and in the future and developing experiences around those assumptions without consultation or experimentation.
- Sticking to traditional, siloed departmental hierarchies, where a project starts off with one team for development until it is ready to move to another team for implementation and then to yet another team to go to market, rather than a flatter, more integrated structure that lends itself to agile decision-making and rapid prototyping.

From Long Time to Market to Quick, Market-Driven Innovation

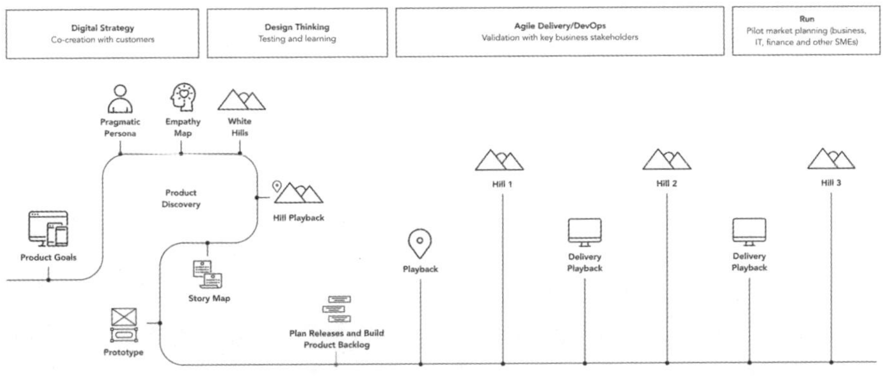

The key take-home message is: do the groundwork to embed design, experience, customer, and culture into the strategy of the business first and let that drive transformation through the use of technology rather than the other way around.

Having reached the end of this chapter, you should now have an understanding of:

- The emerging trends that are shaping markets and influencing the survival of today's businesses.

- The need for companies to evolve to meet the challenges of those emerging trends.
- Why digital transformation is not just about upgrading your website and moving the way you do business onto the cloud.

Stay tuned! In chapter two, we'll consider in more detail the role design plays in organizational transformation past, present, and future and why it matters for continued business success.

CHAPTER 2

DESIGN MATTERS—HISTORY AND EVOLUTION

> *"Design must reflect the practical and aesthetic in business, but above all, good design must primarily serve people."*
>
> —Thomas J. Watson

Every day, we interact with objects, products, services, and people. These interactions not only allow us to live our daily lives but also to connect with people, places, and goods.

These interactions are always the result of someone trying to generate an action, or an intention, and they are designed! Even the simplest thing, like holding a cup of tea, is the result of design. The cup holder is there to generate interaction—in this case, helping you avoid getting your hands burnt when the tea is hot. This was designed to generate that effect.

Definition of Design

From Wikipedia:

A design is a plan or specification for the construction of an object or system or for the implementation of an activity or process, or the result of that plan or specification in the form of a prototype, product or process. The verb to design expresses the process of developing a design. In some cases, the direct construction of an object without an explicit prior plan (such as in craftwork, some engineering, coding and graphic design) may also be considered to be a design activity. The design usually has to satisfy certain goals and constraints, may take into account aesthetic, functional, economic or socio-political considerations and is expected to interact with a certain environment. Major examples of designs include architectural blueprints, engineering drawings, business processes, circuit diagrams and sewing patterns.[4]

My definition:

Design is the relationship that governs the interaction between entities.

[4] "Design," Wikipedia, https://en.wikipedia.org/wiki/Design.

For years, executives and corporations have associated design with the cosmetic and aesthetic element of "how things look." Design has been regarded as an art—sometimes too crazy and abstract to be understood. Corporations then have opted to see design as a way to "enrich" their value propositions, to make them more saleable and more attractive.

However, design is much more than how things look. It is not just a cosmetic element that comes at the end of the creation process. It is not just "art." Design is a driving element of behavior, which can be used to shape business visions into experiences that can really transform organizations and industries.

Anyone can create a beautiful design. But the important thing is that we create a design that drives behavior—that helps you, as an organization, achieve the goals and objectives that you have for your business. Design must fulfill a need and must be compelling in the way that it can be consumed. We also need to think about the usage and the end user of that design. On the one hand, we can be extremely focused on the brand; on the other hand, we can concentrate on the customer.

Think how the design of a ketchup bottle has changed. Instead of having to flip the bottle upside down, tap it on the bottom, and hope some ketchup emerges, now you simply squeeze the bottle, and out comes the ketchup. This is an example of design focused on the end user rather than the brand. We can say that design is a creative activity that must deliver objects that are useful and aesthetic.

Now that we've established that, let's go back in time together to examine the history of design. As we continue through this chapter, we will consider the evolving impact of design from the Industrial Revolution through to the start-ups revolution. By comprehensively understanding design, we can unlock a crucial tool to create new value propositions and discover why it is critical to the success of your business.

Design and the Industrial Revolution

Prior to the Industrial Revolution, manual laborers learned their trade by going through an apprenticeship under a master craftsman, often taking years to progress from novice to master. Most production depended on water, wind, or human energy, and the businesses that existed were known as cottage industries. This term reflected the fact that most goods were produced in limited quantities by workers in their own homes.

By the mid-1700s, new methods of production were being developed, leading to the factory system. These new factories became centralized in industrial towns and cities. By the late eighteenth and early nineteenth centuries, automation by machines was introduced, driven by the improvement in the steam engine and its integration into manufacturing. Steam had the ability to power large machines capable of producing goods in large quantities at low prices.

The manufacture of textiles is an example of this shift from a cottage industry to factory-based production. Before steam, the manufacture of textiles was performed on a limited scale by workers in their own homes or workshops. Spinning and weaving were still done in households for domestic consumption, and any surplus was sold to clothiers passing through the village or town and sold on.

The mechanization of the textile industry through the introduction of new steam-driven machines replaced the craftsmen, resulting in faster and cheaper production but often sacrificing the quality of the product. In fact, The Great Exhibition of the Works of Industry of All Nations in London in 1851 drew criticism for the shoddy and poorly designed products created by these industrialized methods.

Timeline of the Industrial Revolution

This revolution in industry meant that machines were now crafting the goods while the worker's role had become much less specialized. It was more concerned with feeding machines the raw materials they needed to deliver the final product than producing the product themselves. At this time, we can say that design:

- Provided solutions to manufacturing problems.
- Focused on the mass production of goods.
- Used automated factories.

We can also say that this was often to the detriment of the product.

There was no thought given to using design to provide solutions for people's lives. Industrial products were no longer being crafted but designed using a template and then mass produced. The designer was no longer a craftsman but someone who created the templates and planned the production process while the machine and factory workers implemented the design. In essence, products were planned by designers and engineers and then manufactured by machines and unskilled workers. This separation became referred to as **industrial design**.

The arts and crafts movement of the early 1900s, while opposing the tradeoff between fast, efficient production and quality craftsmanship, did recognize that industrially manufactured goods also had the potential to create durable and aesthetic products for the general population.

This became particularly evident in the second stage of the industrial revolution when steam was replaced with electricity and a new type of product entered people's households: the electric appliance. This provided a unique challenge for designers and required a different approach: **product design**.

The first iterations of these electric-powered products presented new technology in old, familiar designs. A new electric kettle looked very similar to the old, familiar stove kettle. This made it easier for the user to understand, accept, and buy into the product. "It's like your old one but better" was the main design message.

Probably the best (and most recognizable) example of large-scale manufacturing epitomized by the Industrial Revolution that still continues today is that of car manufacturing. Henry Ford combined car building with assembly line manufacturing and changed the automobile industry forever. The establishment of the Ford Motor Company in June 1903 was the beginning of a technological revolution in both automotive design and manufacturing techniques.

At the start, Ford built cars the same way as everybody else—one at a time. The vehicle was assembled from the chassis up in one spot on the factory floor with workers sourcing parts from stores in other parts of the factory before returning to fit them. To speed up the process, the component parts were assembled on benches, and the chassis was moved from one team of workers to the next for fitting. However, this was still time consuming, requiring skilled teams of mechanics. Essentially, the car was being hand built.

For Ford to achieve his goal of mass consumption through mass production, the next step was automation. Ford and his engineers invented machines to make large quantities of the parts needed for the vehicle and devised methods of assembling parts as fast as they were made. Workers were placed at appointed stations, and the chassis was hauled along between them, stopping at each station for parts to be fitted before being passed on to the next station and so on until the car was complete.

The creation of a moving assembly line system vastly improved production efficiency. Instead of the factory workers moving around to the parts, they stayed in one place, and the vehicle was brought to them via the assembly line. The company had multiple rails set up inside the factory, and the cars, starting with the chassis and axle, were moved along the track to the next set of workers trained in their particular part of the operation. Once that station had completed their tasks, the car would move on, and the workers would wait for the next vehicle to come along.

In this way, the Ford Motor Company was able to produce more cars more quickly, and the price became more affordable. Owning a car was no longer limited to the rich; everyone could enjoy the benefits of car ownership, with the Model T being dubbed "the car that put the world on wheels!"

But that wasn't where the transformation stopped. Workers found the repetitive nature of the assembly line and their part in it both tiring and boring. In order to retain workers and incentivize others to return, Ford transformed the working week itself, moving from the traditional six-day workweek to a five-day week and doubling the pay. These changes to the working week, coupled with an eight-hour day plus holiday and sick pay, shook up the manufacturing industry.

Ford's assembly line techniques spread, making high-wage, low-skilled jobs common throughout the sector. Through design, both of the car and the manufacturing process, Henry Ford changed the way people work, build, and design forever. The assembly line at the first Ford factory in Michigan became the benchmark for mass production methods around the world.

While industrial and product design still focused on tangible, physical artifacts and material things, the emergence of electronics and information technology meant that the new field of **graphic design** began to explore the use of visual symbols and how to communicate information through words and images.

The introduction of the printing press was the initial step on the graphic design journey. Book designer William Addison Dwiggins first used the term to describe exactly what his role in structuring and managing the visuals in book design entailed.

Throughout the 1900s, posters—most notably, the 1940s propaganda posters—became the most common form of graphic design expression. Slogans were short and to the point and added a graphic to set the tone. As technology evolved and became available to more people, the entire industry that became known as graphic design took shape.

The Industrial Revolution encompassed three distinct but interconnected phases: industrial design, product design, and graphic design. All were driven by the evolution of technology either through steam, electronics, or information technology. By the 1950s, however, the world had started its slow approach to the digital era we know today via the computer revolution.

Design and the Computer Revolution

Following the success of the Industrial Revolution, companies, designers, and engineers continued along the path of automating the production process. With this focus, the need for even more autonomous machines and the ability to "compute" paved the way for the computer revolution. This revolution of design was largely driven by the personal computer and the development of the internet. It was characterized by the advancement of technology from analog, electronic, and mechanical devices to digital technology.

During the 1970s and '80s, cheap, fast computing, affordable disk storage, and networking became more widely available. Standalone personal computers were predominantly used for gaming and word processing. At the same time, the idea of open-source development and collaboration gained traction in university computer science departments with common operating systems, programming languages, and tools.

As these networks spread, tools that were developed in one place could be shared and used in another. The networks became more uniform and interlinked, creating a digital traffic infrastructure—in other words, a global internet. With the increasing storage capacity, systems became libraries of information as opposed to just being used for conversations between networks via email and chat forums. This library could be accessed globally and used as an exchange for data and code.

In 1990, researchers at CERN created a system for storing documents and publishing them to the internet, which they named the World Wide Web. As a result of this global sharing, documents were increasingly being written specifically for online publication, and web pages were born.

In comparison to research and education settings, computers set up in businesses at this time tended to be customized, isolated, and rigid. However, by the mid-1990s, internet commerce was a growing sector of the global economy with the internet allowing easy access to information and easy trade for goods and services. Companies keen to capitalize on this started developing websites.

Web design required a different thought process to ensure the user could navigate easily through the site and activate hypertext links to jump to additional information or content. It presented a whole new set of design challenges, not least moving away from the Microsoft Disk Operating System (MS-DOS) interface where users typed commands line by line onto a black screen.

The increasing use of personal computers led graphic designers to introduce the graphical user interface (GUI). This used pictures and images to control programs through icons, buttons, and pointers, something that could easily be customized for business websites. The changing ways users interacted with software, from programming languages to command line interfaces and finally through GUIs, is wholly down to design.

Probably the most recognizable example of the changing face of design through the computer revolution is that of Microsoft. Microsoft's first standalone setup required only three components: a keyboard for input, a monitor for output, and a personal computer (PC) to run the operating system. At this point, graphic design wasn't even a consideration. The only way to tell the computer what you wanted it to do was to type text commands into the command line using a suitable programming language.

It was the introduction of the mouse as a new way to interact with the operating system that heralded the arrival of the GUI. This meant that instead of typing in instructions, users now moved the mouse and clicked on the symbol of the task they wanted to perform. Interestingly, Microsoft found their engineers were now seeking out the help of print designers as the importance of the user interface both for software development and competitive advantage became apparent.

By 1990, as typography technology improved and online fonts were standardized, Microsoft saw huge increases in sales of their Windows operating system. The launch of Windows 95 demonstrated the impact design was having on Microsoft's success and differentiation from others in the market. It was the first time users experienced the now familiar start button and task bar, and in the first five weeks, it sold seven million copies.

By the late 1990s, due in no small part to Microsoft, it was commonplace for businesses to operate using the internet, and we saw the dotcom boom emerge as the true paradox between online and digital business. The statement was clear: The future was online, and any company that wanted to survive had to be on the internet.

The whole understanding of the world at that time was that digital interactions would replace physical interactions. Even air travel was seen as something highly likely to decline, as people replaced the need for traveling with utilizing digital means like videoconferencing. As such, almost every company, particularly the brick-and-mortar ones, started pursuing a digital business.

However, by the year 2000, the lack of compelling value propositions, along with costly technology and poor user experiences, ended the dotcom boom. The bubble burst, and with that, so too did many companies' single focus of going online. During the years that followed, companies turned their back on digital, returning to their traditional way of doing business and neglecting online as something with no future at all.

That was the rebirth of brick and mortar, which refocused on the vertical and horizontal integration of businesses while bringing into the equation a new concept: user-centric store design. Yes, designing a store around customer behavior and, more importantly, using the store as something that could extend the experience beyond the purchase of a product.

Thus, bookstores became coffee shops and places to browse and explore books; consumer electronic stores became playgrounds to experience new products; and large retailers mastered the store-in-store concept as a way to expand their offerings. It was the surge of a new way to shop—a retailer aiming to establish a connection with its customers, with design at its heart.

So far, our design journey has taken us from the Industrial Revolution, where design aimed to replicate existing products but in larger quantities, to the start of the computer revolution, where this too was the main driver of design. Many digital products and services were simply faster or more efficient versions of analog technology. Effectively, the word processor was the digital equivalent of a typewriter.

But at this point, designers and the work of design started to move in a new direction. Instead of designing systems to replicate manual labor, designers were looking to design systems that replicated intellectual labor. Computing was moving from being simply fed by human-inputted data streams—traffic data, weather data, banking transactions—to computer learning and modeling.

Computers have since become embedded in our lives with sensors and actuators everywhere. The infrastructure is being built into the environment, and cloud computing is becoming an accepted necessity along the same lines as water and electricity. Through social media, computing also acts as social currency to create and consolidate social relationships.

This proliferation and the opportunities it creates bring us to the next stage in the design journey: the start-ups revolution. This was driven by the evolution of technology and built upon the increasing acceptance of the importance of design in the development of new value propositions. These start-ups leveraged both elements to further fuel their proposals, gaining traction, market share, and ultimately size.

Design and the Start-Ups Revolution—Digital as the Key Enabler

While retailers were focusing on building a physical relationship with customers, a few companies that survived the dotcom burst, along with new ones that aimed to create value propositions based on still unanswered needs, were using digital technologies to create a more intimate relationship with their customers, getting to know them better to further personalize their offerings and to deliver an entire experience designed for individuals. As such, a few companies like Amazon and Expedia started to build a new market—one based on the power of analytics and enabled technologies with the capability to cater and personalize an experience.

A great example of this is the Amazon app. The entire app has been created and conceived with the end user at the center of it and with a clear intent of driving and completing purchases. It allows easy integration across platforms, scanning of desired products, and up-sale and cross-sale. Even more relevant, it offers a simple and straightforward checkout and payment system, which entices and enables a great customer experience that boosts the utilization of the app and drives business success.

Other companies took the opportunity presented by the advancement of technology—as well as the reducing cost of that technology—to turn themselves into format invaders, expanding beyond their core business model and jumping into areas completely outside their original capabilities. Every business has its own way of organizing the many activities involved in delivering its product or service—in other words, its format.

Format invaders come along with a new way of doing business. They reexamine the activities common across the industry or discover a completely new way of performing them, often with technology at its heart. This may entail reducing the cost base but can also involve redesigning the way you engage with the customer.

Consider the fuel retail sector. The predominant format in the past has been large, self-service petrol stations combined with a convenience store. Format invaders are changing this.

For example, in Scandinavia, completely unattended petrol stations are being introduced. They're a bit like a petrol vending machine, which means diminished costs, particularly in staffing, resulting in increased margins. In the UK and elsewhere in Europe, supermarkets are taking on the role of format invaders by adding petrol stations to their stores and leveraging their existing assets to offer petrol at much lower prices. Essentially, petrol is just another product on their metaphorical shelf!

The original format invaders used technology and their ability to build value propositions catered to a specific well-segmented individual to drive business success. However, as the world continued to evolve and a new generation—millennials—emerged, the use of technology started to facilitate new social interactions, which crossed the digital and physical divide. All sorts of applications arose, utilizing physical location to allow customized interactions. More importantly, customers demanded physical interaction, that "real" human engagement in the shopping process, but this time combined with the best of technology in order to make the interaction unique.

This massive behavioral change has forced online retailers to desperately expand into a physical presence. Today, both Amazon and eBay, the two pinnacles of online retailing, are opening physical stores, aiming for that unique connection with customers that can only happen in the real world. Thus, retailers have the unique opportunity to leverage digital technologies to create new ways to engage with their customers in their physical stores.

This challenge has only intensified with the emergence of COVID-19. By necessity, the pandemic accelerated digital adoption and drove a change in consumer behavior that meant *all* physical interactions had to be meaningful. Remote working, travel restrictions, and a new work/life balance all challenged the traditional way of doing business. Concerns about transmission meant that both organizations and customers became more careful about the people and products they interacted with. Everyone had to seriously decide whether an interaction really needed to be in person, face to face, or if it could be done as effectively, and perhaps more safely, digitally.

One such company forced to reevaluate the way it did business was the cosmetics company Lin Qingxuan in China. Having closed 40 percent of its stores due to COVID-19, they redeployed their one hundred-plus store-based beauty advisors to become online influencers, leveraging digital chat technology to engage with customers and drive online sales. The result? A 200 percent growth in sales year on year in Wuhan alone.

This changing nature of design means that it is now much more related to experiences and interactions centered around people. Every time you put something out there, every time you create a product, the expectations of your customers are evolving, and those expectations never stop.

Many companies create an amazing and beautiful customer interface that then fails to integrate with the back end or fails to integrate with the operations. It's not enough to focus on one part of the interaction; you need to focus on the *entire* interaction.

And here's where the transformation part comes in. No longer are we simply designing a product or a service. Now, we are designing an experience. We take a product or service that has been around for many years, and we transform it into a completely new experience.

This change has been driven by the disruptors, those companies that started with zero value as a start-up of two or three people in a garage without the limitations that most midsized to big corporations have. They are focused exclusively on creating the best product or service to put into the market. That focus excels when it comes to design and allows them to disrupt the market in multiple ways through prototyping and iterative learning.

3 Digital Disruptors That Grew During the COVID-19 Pandemic

zoom

Disruptor 1
Revolutionized remote communication with its easy-to-use video conferencing platform, becoming essential for businesses, education, and social interactions.

NETFLIX

Disruptor 2
Saw a significant increase in subscriptions as people sought entertainment while confined to their homes.

amazon

Disruptor 3
Expanded its dominance in e-commerce and cloud computing, becoming a critical service for home delivery and remote work solutions.

Design and Value Propositions

Design is about the interaction we're trying to build with the product or service. However, the most important thing is that we create design that drives behavior and helps you as an organization achieve your unique goals.

Design must fulfill a need, and that need must be contained in a way that can be consumed. The move from designing for function to designing for humans means that the concept of design is now concerned with the process of discovering goals, learning what matters, and entering into a conversation between parties to develop a desired outcome. In the future, design will be concerned with complex systems and environments for living, working, playing, and learning. It has truly moved on from providing manufacturing solutions to finding solutions for people's lives.

Prescription glasses company Warby Parker is a great example of putting design at the center of the value proposition. Founded in 2010, Warby Parker hit their one-year sales target in just three weeks. How? By listening to what the market was telling them.

They created an online store, which removed the cost of maintaining traditional retail locations and meant their glasses could be sold at significantly lower prices. And they introduced an interactive showroom where customers could virtually try on the glasses and share via social media. Early adopters were so pleased with the design, purchasing experience, and overall value that they told their family, friends, and work colleagues to the extent that over half of all Warby Parker's new customers came via word-of-mouth referrals.

However, increasingly, they were getting feedback that their customers actually really valued the in-person shopping experience. So with customer satisfaction high on their priority list, Warby Parker decided to create a series of brick-and-mortar stores to complement their virtual showroom. This allowed for the personal interaction their customers valued and the instant gratification of trying on and buying the glasses in real time. The difference between Warby Parker and the traditional retailers of glasses was that they created small but efficient locations by utilizing modern technology.

In addition, they provided opportunities for their customers to be part of a solution to improve other people's lives. Research studies have found that the majority of consumers now place a higher value on brands that contribute to a wider purpose.

From the start, Warby Parker had placed an emphasis on charitable donations to those in need. One particular initiative—buy a pair, give a pair—allowed their customers to do the same, gifting over five million pairs of glasses to individuals across the world. By listening to the market, being flexible in responding to feedback, and designing for the needs of humans, they have fundamentally changed the value proposition found in the eyewear industry.

Warby Parker's success is that they understand consumer behavior and trends. Not only do they design and deliver a beautiful product for a fraction of the cost of traditional eyewear retailers, but their social mission has positioned them ideally for growth in their millennial customer base, as they are more likely to make purchasing decisions based on a brand's social impact than on cost alone.

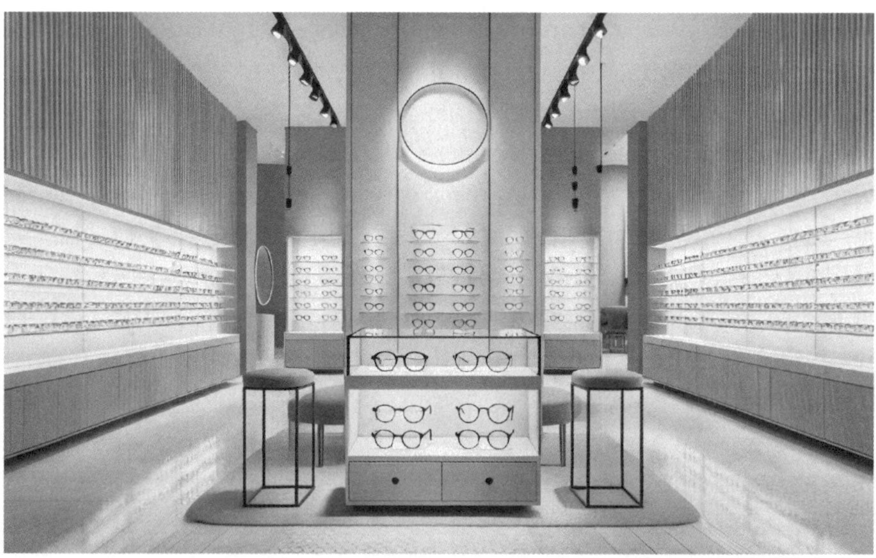

The example of Warby Parker helps demonstrate an important paradigm shift where design is no longer an aesthetic component but rather an exigent driver of human behavior. Design has transcended users' mere functional utility through interaction with the designed artifacts. Instead, it is an embodiment of empathy with users' underlying emotions and motivations and a trigger of predicted behaviors that ultimately drives business outcomes.

The way we design is not only a representation of what we are as a business—our values and beliefs—but also our business objectives. Our approach to design and then the execution of that design in the form of value propositions is to effectively change the behavior of our customers and employees. By crafting an original *designed* value proposition, we are then able to drive our clients into the right interactions that will create the most valuable outcome for them and our own enterprises.

From physical layout to the latest digital application, design is driving behaviors and business results across industries and domains. Thus, design is a hidden gem that, most of the time, is undervalued. Further, it is one of the key success factors of any business in today's changing world.

The best design environments encourage learning, testing, and iterating with users to boost the odds of creating breakthrough products and services. Early sharing of prototypes outside the company and recognition that the product launch isn't the end of the design process is what differentiates the successful start-up from incumbent businesses.

The constant cycle of updating, tweaking, and improvement once the product or service is out in the "real world" is what characterizes these disruptors. It requires customer insight gathered by observing and understanding the underlying needs of potential users in their own environments. But more than that, it is a deep appreciation for what users need rather than what they say they want.

The start-up revolution demonstrated how, through fast access to real customers via social media and smart devices, consumers can be placed at the heart of business decisions. Unfortunately, many traditional businesses have been slow to catch up, with studies showing over 40 percent of companies are still not talking to their end users during development.

Many organizations still do not see a clear link between design and the bottom line, so let's take a look at why investing in design is crucial to the financial success of your business.

Design Is Crucial to Financial Success

"What business needs now is design. What design needs now is making it about business."

—Beth Comstock, SVP GE and
co-chair, DMI conference 2011

Design is a key differentiator in driving business success and customer engagement. The business value of design has been studied extensively and shows a powerful return on virtually all measures for those companies consciously using design as part of their business strategy.

The McKinsey Design Index (MDI) rated companies based on their financial performance and found those with higher MDI scores correlated with higher revenue growth and financial outperformance across all three industries studied (medical technology, consumer goods, and retail banking). The best design performers increased their revenues and shareholder returns, outperforming industry benchmarks by as much as two to one. These results were found in all three of the industries studied, suggesting that good design matters whether your business is in physical goods or digital products or services. In short, the results indicated that the better the company was at using design as an integral part of their business, the higher the growth revenue and the higher the returns to shareholders.

The MDI is not alone in coming to this conclusion. In Europe, the UK Design Council study of design-led firms found that for every one pound spent on design, companies saw an increase in revenue of more than twenty pounds, an increase in profit of four pounds, and a five-pound increase in exports. That's right—for every one pound spent on design, there was a corresponding and significant increase in revenue, profit, and exports.

Similar findings were reported in the 2018 Design Delivers report by the Design Danish Centre. Sixty-seven percent of companies using design saw their competitiveness improve, 60 percent sold more products/services, and 92 percent reported a positive impact on their bottom line. This indicates that choosing to invest in design will positively and dramatically impact the financial success of your business.

What about stock performance? The Design Management Institute (DMI) Design Value Index tracked how design-centric companies performed between 2003 and 2013 relative to the Standard and Poor's (S&P). Fifteen publicly traded companies passed a rigorous test of design-led management criteria, and over the ten years, these companies maintained significant stock market advantage, outperforming the S&P by 228 percent. This clearly demonstrates a strong correlation between organizations that invest in design and extraordinary stock performance.

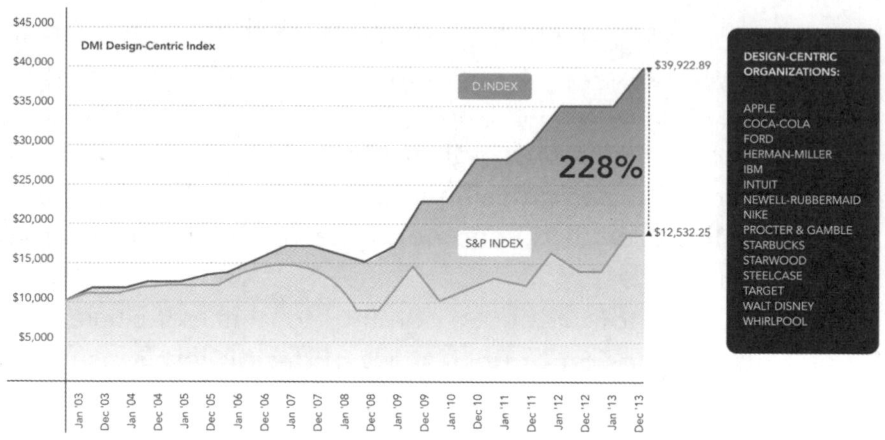

Not only is the economic value of design clear, but it also contributes positively to non-economic or non-financial gains. In a worldwide design maturity study across 2,200 companies and twenty-four industries, it was shown that design enabled 81 percent of businesses to have improved product useability, 71 percent to deliver higher customer satisfaction, and all to demonstrate improved employee productivity by an average of 33 percent.

All this research adds weight to the fact that businesses with a focus on design add significant value both to their financial and non-financial measures. These companies are using design to connect more deeply with their users, customers, and collaborators and, as a result, are boosting their competitive advantage.

Remember, design-centric businesses are design-led. They put design at the core of their brand and in everything they do from research and strategy to creating content and managing internal processes. Not only that, but from the top down, they think beyond a transactional relationship with their customer and focus on creating experiences in order to build a meaningful and ongoing customer relationship.

Good design is the difference between a complex, frustrating interaction and a delightful experience. Well-designed interactions can save us time and make us more productive. Consider how often you close a website in frustration because it isn't mobile friendly. Or on the flip side, think about when you use an app on your smartphone that allows you to do exactly what you want, when you want, in three clicks. This highlights the importance of good design and the difference design thinking can play in your organization.

In 2018, IBM commissioned a report to look at the total economic impact of their design thinking practice. To clarify, design thinking places end users at the center of the design process, and IBM has used this principle across the organization's diverse portfolio of products and services to help clients cut costs, increase speed, and design better solutions. The report aimed to evaluate design thinking's financial impact for both individual, standalone projects and the transformation of the wider organization. The results?

- Human-centered design improved product outcomes, lowered the risk of costly failures, and increased portfolio profitability to the tune of 18.6 million dollars.
- Project teams doubled design and execution speed, resulting in accelerated project delivery, thus reducing costs by 20.6 million dollars.
- Time to market was twice as quick, meaning increased profits of between 182 thousand dollars for smaller projects and 1.1 million dollars for larger ones.
- Cross-functional teams collaborated to share problems and find solutions, reducing costs by 9.2 million dollars in streamlined processes.

In addition to these financial measures, the study revealed considerable benefits of design thinking to non-economic factors:

- An empowered, engaged, and happy workforce.
- Enhanced key performance indicators (KPIs), including user interface, user experience, customer experience, net promoter score, and brand energy.
- Perfected internal processes for departments such as HR and sales.

The take-home message is clear: if you want to transform your business, you need to put design at the center of everything you do.

To recap, throughout this chapter, we have explored the following:

- The impact of design on the industrial revolution.
- Its effect on the computer revolution.
- How design has driven the start-up revolution by creating new value propositions.
- Both financial and non-financial reasons why becoming a design-centric business is crucial to your organization's success.

Stick with me—in chapter three, we will explore how you can create these experiences using user-centric, analytically informed design.

CHAPTER 3

DESIGNING EXPERIENCES

"There's no technology that can be 'The Answer' to a better customer experience in the absence of effective strategy and planning."

—Brad Cleveland

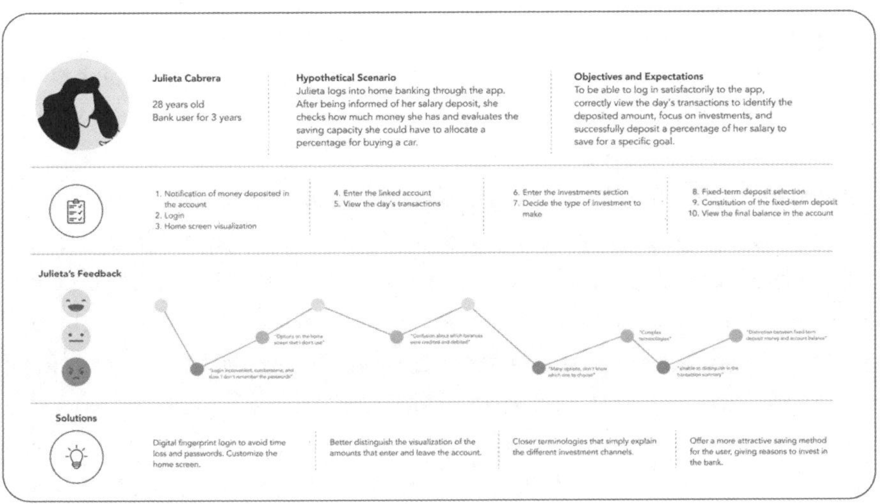

In the previous chapters, we discussed the new drivers that are shaping our world and examined the importance of design. In this chapter, we will continue our journey toward transforming organizations powered by design. To do so, we will address one of the most relevant components of digital transformation: the experience. We will refer to experience as the actual process and result of deriving and composing a customer experience.

Customer experience encompasses every aspect of a company's offerings—not only the quality of the customer care but also the advertising, packaging, product and service features, ease of use, and reliability. In traditional product businesses, product development defers to marketing when it comes to customer experience issues, and both have historically focused on features and specifications. This must change!

Even the service industry is not immune to the subdivision of responsibility for customer experience. Customer service personnel tend to focus on the current transaction with the customer—"Is there anything else I can help you with today?"—rather than the wider connection to the customer both preceding and following that transaction. They may not even have resolved the original reason for the interaction but will still go on to ask the standard signing-off question.

Interestingly, many companies believe they are consistently giving customers what they want. A study of over 360 companies, conducted by Bain & Company, revealed that 80 percent believed they provided a "superior experience" to their customers. And yet, when their customers were asked the same question, they said only 8 percent of firms were really delivering.

Consumers have a greater number of choices today than ever before and more channels through which to pursue them. This means that businesses urgently need to better understand their time-pressed customers in order to survive.

You may be one of many companies that already measure customer satisfaction, but the problem is that won't tell you how to achieve it. In essence, customer satisfaction is the culmination of customer experiences. Good experiences add to the customer satisfaction score, and bad experiences detract from it. Closing the gap between your customers' expectations and their subsequent experiences increases your satisfaction score.

The difficulty comes when you realize that many customer experiences aren't a direct result of the brand's message. They encompass the internal and subjective responses customers have to any direct or indirect contact with your company. This might be in the course of purchasing a product or using your service (direct contact). Or it might be word-of-mouth recommendations/criticisms, news reports, or reviews (indirect contact). This is why it is so important to understand the difference between customer relationship management and customer experience management.

Customer relationship management (CRM) is concerned with what the company knows about their customers and generally occurs as a result of customer interactions. In contrast, **customer experience management (CEM)** is concerned with what a customer thinks about the company and is captured at points of customer interaction or "touchpoints." The benefit of the latter approach is that it allows you to identify the opportunity to close the gap between a consumer's expectation and their experience. CRM tracks customers' actions after the fact, and CEM captures the immediate response of the customer to their encounters or interactions with the company.

This is particularly crucial when you consider that customer interactions are now more social in nature, and peer customers are also influencing experiences. We can certainly say that customer-to-customer interactions through social media are creating significant challenges and opportunities for organizations. Establishing strong, positive experiences within the customer journey will result in improvements to the bottom line by enhancing performance in the customer journey at multiple touchpoints (i.e., higher conversion rates) and through improved customer loyalty as well as increased word-of-mouth recommendations.

However, let's take a step back and consider the concept of customer experience. It's certainly a dynamic process encompassing the customer's journey with a business over time from prepurchase (including search) through purchase to post-purchase across multiple touchpoints. And only some of these touchpoints are within the company's control.

Secondly, the key to fully appreciating the meaning of customer experience is to understand that consumers value experiences more than goods and services. Experiences are memorable events that engage each individual in an inherently personal way. They are not a new economic offering (think theatres, music concerts, and art galleries); they are an untapped means of differentiation.

Although experiences themselves lack tangibility, people greatly desire them because their value lies within them, where it remains long after the actual experience has ended. In fact, studies have shown that buying experiences makes people happier and gives them a greater sense of well-being than purchasing goods or services alone. In effect, people prefer experiences over commodities and doing over having.

Every company today competes with every other company for the time, attention, and money of potential customers. What this means in practice is that every business, whether product or service driven, needs to create an experience that first gains potential customers' attention. Then, they must get them to spend time experiencing what the company has to offer and finally cause them to spend their money by buying those offerings.

Goods and services are no longer enough in the "experience economy" to deliver economic growth, create new jobs, and maintain economic prosperity. Apple is a case in point.

Prior to creating their revolutionary new retail format, Apple studied the hospitality experiences at high-end boutique hotels for design inspiration. The subsequent store design and the experience they deliver are more like a town square or community meeting place than a store or retail unit. In fact, Apple has removed "store" from the names of its new locations to ensure both customers and employees focus on the Apple experience rather than buying a product from a shop shelf. The community aspect has taken center stage with Apple locations being a place to gather, learn, and be entertained.

The most salient point this example raises is that a technology company is investing in experiences that bring people together, not virtually but in reality. More and more people are bringing their technological devices (iPods, iPhones, iPads, etc.) with them wherever they go; therefore, companies need to fuse the virtual and the real world together to create new digitally infused experiences. This may mean greater integration of the digital into the physical, but it may also mean removing digital devices that intrude on the face-to-face interaction.

So in answer to the question "What is customer experience?" we can say it is the sum of the interactions that make up the thinking, feeling, and doing of a person before, during, and after they've interacted with a product or service. This forms the experience and connections made between the company and its users, creating a positive or negative presence in decision-making, which transcends the transaction. It is often confused with user experience and user interface, which are indeed related but only make up part of the total consumer experience.

Remember, the customer experience is the perception customers have of a brand shaped by all interactions, both direct and indirect. It encompasses every touchpoint, from friend recommendations and purchases to emails, invoices, phone or chatbot conversations, and exposure to advertising on social media, billboards, or TV. On the other hand, user interface refers to the graphical and navigational design of each digital interaction. In the case of an app, it involves designing the visual elements and navigation from screen to screen, ensuring a seamless and visually appealing user interface within the broader customer experience.

We must also consider the value proposition, offer, market trends, marketing, customer service, and all direct and indirect points of contact with the consumer. Customer experience must be the main focus of organizations. Always put the client at the center of strategic decisions—for real! Despite what almost every organization on the planet claims, just a few of them really consider the customer when devising strategies, creating new offerings, or developing a retention strategy for customers seeking to terminate the services a company is providing.[5]

---

[5] "New and diverse experiences linked to enhanced happiness, new study shows," US National Science Foundation, June 2, 2020, https://new.nsf.gov/news/new-diverse-experiences-linked-enhanced-happiness.

In addition, organizations need to understand that the customer experience and customer journey they define will be constantly evolving as customers and markets evolve. As such, their strategies need to be dynamic and evolutionary and must be adapted to each type of client to fulfill the singular requirement of personalized experiences. Now, it is the customer who has the upper hand as they not only seek better prices but focus on the experience that the brand can deliver.

Indeed, a study carried out by the English company Clarabridge found that:

- Fifty-five percent of shoppers would pay more for a better shopping experience service, but only 1 percent of them believe that companies know their expectations.
- Eighty-nine percent of consumers stop doing business with a company after going through a bad service experience.

It's often said that experience is the result of all the actions and interactions that a business or enterprise generates. However, we understand experience as the intention. Thus, since experience is an intention and therefore an objective, not a result, it can and should be designed!

Evolution from Product Centric to Customer Centric

Fifty-four percent of global executives believe that customer buying behavior is shifting from product/service to experience.

Experience changes all—experience *is* all. Consider the difference between the following two images. One is all about the product; the other is all about the experience the product can give you.

Transform this: To this:

Another good illustration of "experience is all" is the story of the designer who created the MRI machine pictured below:

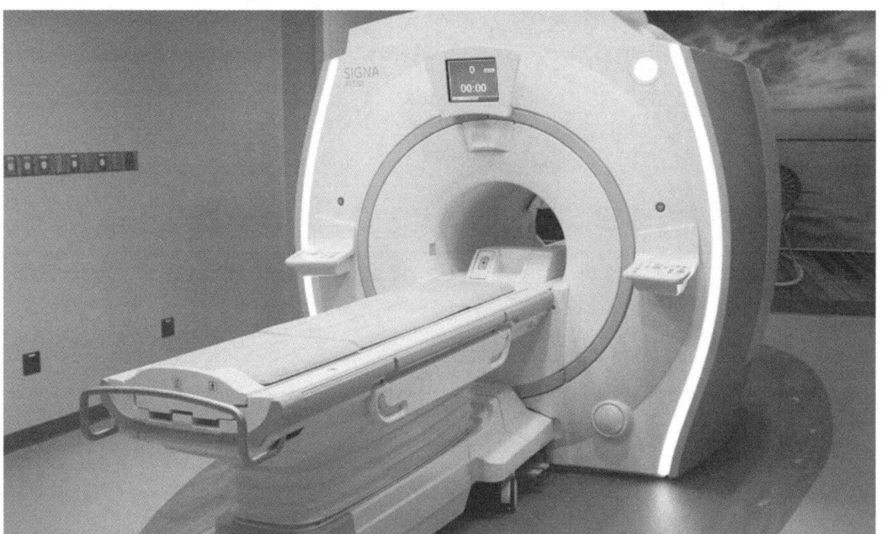

Terrible!
GE MRI machine

He was very comfortable and proud of the work he had done until a family friend's young son had to go for an MRI scan. The little boy was scared—scared of the process and scared of the big, noisy machine he was expected to lie still in while he was scanned.

Looking at the MRI machine through the little boy's eyes, the designer realized he had designed it while thinking about the doctors and nurses who had to operate it as well as the hospital management who had to locate it and fund it. In doing so, he had neglected to consider the patient who had to experience it.

So he went back to the drawing board to design an experience for the little boy having his MRI scan, transforming it from an ordeal to get through to an adventure that could be enjoyed. He decided to create a theme for the MRI scan, perhaps going into the ocean or a jungle. As part of this, he developed scripts for the doctors and nurses, created uniforms based on the theme, and concocted a whole story similar to those you might find in a theme park.

Now, consider the experience of that little boy going for his MRI scan when he walks into the room and sees this machine:

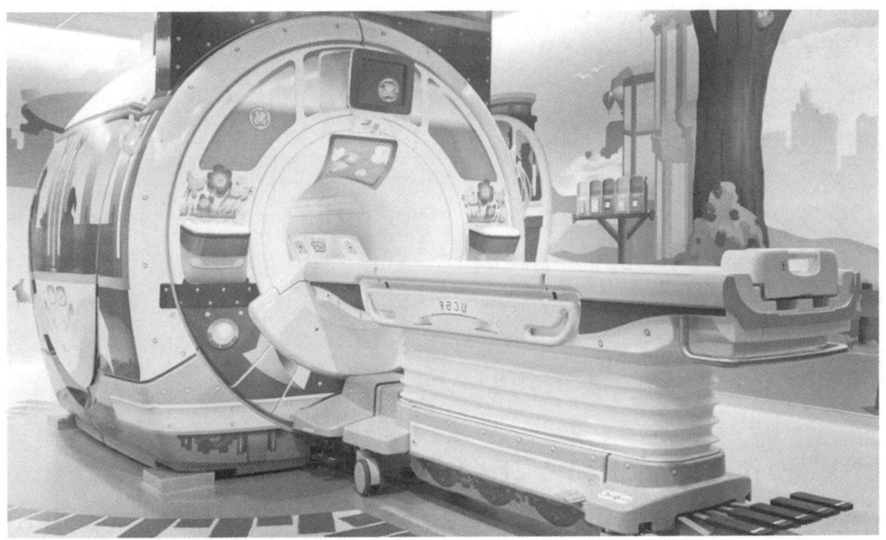

Incredible!
An adventure-themed GE MRI machine

As the intention behind design has changed, the capabilities and talent involved in the design process have also evolved. It's moved from a purely mechanical and functional approach to an experiential and human-centric one created by a pool of experts who center their capabilities on human understanding, situation analysis, and ultimately design and experience. This true multidisciplinary team operates on an iterative basis, learning from the responses that their designs stimulate, then adapting and evolving those designs accordingly. Thus, design becomes an organic system, which, by its nature, evolves dynamically and constantly.

Design-led transformation is the integration of people, processes, methods, principles, and mindsets in the search for human-centered outcomes based on empathy for the people you serve. In every relationship you have with providers of goods and services, there is an inherent end-to-end experience. When designers get involved in creating experiences, they use techniques involving empathy to uncover and optimize for both functional and emotional customer needs.

Designers don't create solutions until they have determined the root issue and then considered the full range of potential solutions. To do that, they need to understand and interpret people and cultures—what is required to capture the hearts and minds of new and target customers and new markets/locations. They must be in touch with both existing and potential customers and be able to identify and fulfill an unmet need. Of course, the ability to engage with a wider variety of customers and cultivate long-term loyalty is crucial.

Intuitive Interactions That Drive Behavior

When we start creating and crafting an experience, we seek to connect our outcome with intuition, which then drives the consumption of those experiences in a singular manner. In that sense, we are able to appreciate that only the most advanced design will effectively drive behavior. It's intuitive—you don't need an explanation; you know immediately how to use it. When the design is so good it pushes you in a certain direction, it encourages an intuitive interaction. There's no manual. You don't need a training course. It's self-explanatory, and that requires a new way of interacting with design.

Much of the literature on how design causes behavior change focuses on a physical store or on a remote online platform or how the future will allow us to interact with anything in our environment digitally. But here's what design enthusiasts should also be asking this: How has human behavior changed over generations to create new demands for flawless experiences? Times have changed only because human behavior has changed. Herein lies the chicken and egg question of whether design causes behavior to change or new thinking and behavior causes design to adapt.

While it is futile to get into origins and first causes, it is safe to say that design and human behavior are intermingling and causing each other to emerge in new modes. What we know for sure is that this intermingling is merging dynamically at such speeds that it is impossible to separate the design and human behavior variables today.

In decades past, businesses focused on customer service as a separate department, which traditionally remained siloed away and was always an after-sales thought. But customer demands for "speaking to the right person" and "help with what solution is best for me" has radically changed the aura of customer service to include the vibe before a purchase is even made. We've now come much further and added the word "experience" to include the behavioral tendencies an individual is drawn to when they engage with a brand.

Designing for Emotion

Another facet of designing for experience is emotion. Design has been impacted by three emotional triggers that human beings consciously utilize to improve quality of life since the turn of the century: ease, safety, and freedom. Design as a medium promises not only a guaranteed right of way but also an entire experience characterized by effortlessness, comfort, and instant access to these emotional triggers.

The ease of conducting transactions to save time, effort, and money while increasing joy, convenience, and happiness is built into world-class brands. When Airbnb says the world is home, they essentially are capitalizing on the millennial behavior of sharing homes, cars, and anything for temporary use. Airbnb makes it easy for them to connect to this desire. The sharing economy is an economy of ease.

Psychological safety is similarly addressed with brands like Ikea, with stores designed to invite families to tour and imagine every possibility for the look of their living spaces first. If an audience does not feel safe, they simply do not engage long term, no matter how beautiful the aesthetics are. As brands incorporate the need for psychological well-being into their design, they create trust where customers know exactly what they will experience when they enter a store or go to a website.

The human need for freedom and choice is innate. People are destined to choose, and the human brain is designed to want. Every behavior is shaped ultimately by what is wanted, hoped for, and aspired to. Design has thus evolved from simply being pleasing to the eye into a phenomenon revolutionizing how people express their freedom of choice.

Amazon.com demonstrates this unequivocally by presenting customers with choices at every click, search term, and product page. This experience creates awareness of their sense of freedom, which brings them back time and again.

It is critical to think about how human desire, especially that of Generation Z born after 1998, is constantly affecting the business ecosystem, which puts design at the forefront of every interaction. Design is a compelling component that enables our deepest desires of sharing, outsourcing, creating, and consuming. Engagement, trust, and loyalty are factors associated with Generation Z's buying behavior and brand affinity.

As we move into new generations, we see that their understanding of design is an integral part of the value proposition. Furthermore, it's the aesthetic of the value proposition combined with its dominant design that makes it desirable for these generations. True examples of these preferences are the evolution of retail and food chains, which now are placing an incredible amount of focus on these components.

As millennials (born roughly between 1981 and 1996), Gen Z (born approximately between 1997 and 2012), and centennials (born after 2012) make their mark in the market, their unique understanding of design becomes integral to the evolving concept of the value proposition. These generational cohorts view the aesthetic aspects of a value proposition as inseparable from its overall appeal. This is exemplified in the transformation of industries such as retail and food chains where an unprecedented emphasis is now placed on the harmonious integration of design components. The shift underscores the acknowledgment that the synergy between aesthetic appeal and dominant design significantly shapes the preferences of millennials, Gen Zers, and centennials as both consumers and collaborators.

In conclusion, design is a driver of emotions, and through emotions, we can establish relations with consumers and employees, which then can move into different forms of engagements, our ultimate goal. In this context, designing to create engagement will be a key asset for companies to endure in the future.

Innovation Builds Experiences

Value Proposition Generation

	Traditional Approach	Experience Design Approach
Conception	Business Centric	End User Needs/Pains
Packaging	Consumable	Adjusted to Market & Context
Iteration	None	Permanent
Marketing	Conversion Game	Value Fit
Focus	Clients/Sales	Audience Build-Up
Value Creation	Direct	Direct & Indirect
Approach	Vertical	Horizontal (Platform)

Innovation is coming up with the solution to a problem, and that solution needs to be something that fundamentally creates value. Keep in mind, value is not always economic, but it will eventually translate into economic value. Put differently, innovation is the process of acknowledging a problem and devising a value proposition that taps into that problem and solves it in a new way.

We can have incremental innovation and really disruptive innovation, but that really depends on the industry and the phase of the development of the product life cycle. With a very mature product, the next wave of innovation is likely to come from something really disruptive, which ends with that product but jumps into the next one. But when products are evolving, we see incremental innovations in the form of features or minor updates that help the product to evolve.

The key to doing this successfully is not about trying to create something that is perfect. It's not about building something that has all the features or that aims to please everyone. You need to go to the core of the problem that you're trying to address and provide a solution for that.

Maybe the solution is not even complete but is just a hint of a solution. Put that into the market and start testing it. It's an incremental process, very different from how big corporations have been working for many years. Don't replicate the tired process of conducting development cycles over years and then launching something that is completely perfect. Instead, aim for a **minimum viable product** and build on that.

The New Fundamentals of Experience-Based Businesses

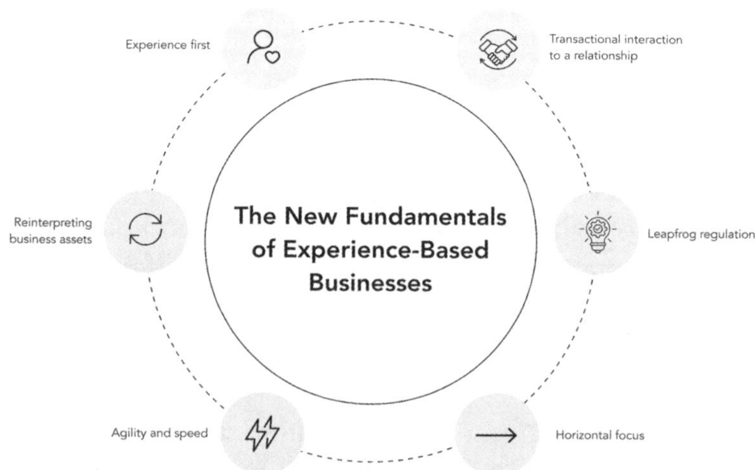

Experience First

The first fundamental is that digital transformation means a focus on the customer and on the collaborator at the center of your value proposition. It's a move from the traditional approach of "I built this product because I think you're going to like it; I'm going to bombard you with marketing messages in order to convince you to buy it, and then I'm going to ship it to you." Instead, it's an attitude of wanting to understand your customer's problems, concerns, and issues and put that at the center of building the product.

From there, you combine it with the business objectives and then build a value proposition. This is just the first iteration. It then goes through a filter—the content landscape, the business landscape, and the regulatory landscape—to determine the value proposition that actually makes it to market. This requires fundamentally changing your thinking to co-creation with your customers and your collaborators based on a business opportunity that lies in the market or in your assets.

Co-creation relies on combined inputs from multidisciplinary teams with target customer profiles front and center to build a customer-centric value proposition. As design-enabling technologies evolve, it becomes easier (and less costly) to prototype, try, tease, and experiment. This gives design the opportunity to not only be at the very beginning of any creation process but to become a continuous input generator as the execution of the design takes place.

This is what we call **continuous co-creation**, where design never really stops, and the same principles of agile iteration development get implemented to design. Design then is no longer a linear sequential process but rather a circular continuous enablement of an experience that is constantly being constructed.

Illustrations of this approach can be extracted from several business examples across industries and domains. In the physical domain, a clear example can be drawn from Starbucks, where design is the driving force of its success.

From the moment a patron enters the coffee shop space, each sensory touchpoint has been carefully conceived to create the cozy experience where coffee (the core product) is merely one of the elements of the entire enjoyment journey. The furniture, the wall art, the background music, the smell of coffee, even the personal touch of writing the customer's name on the cup and calling them out on a first name and friendly basis are part of the experience design.

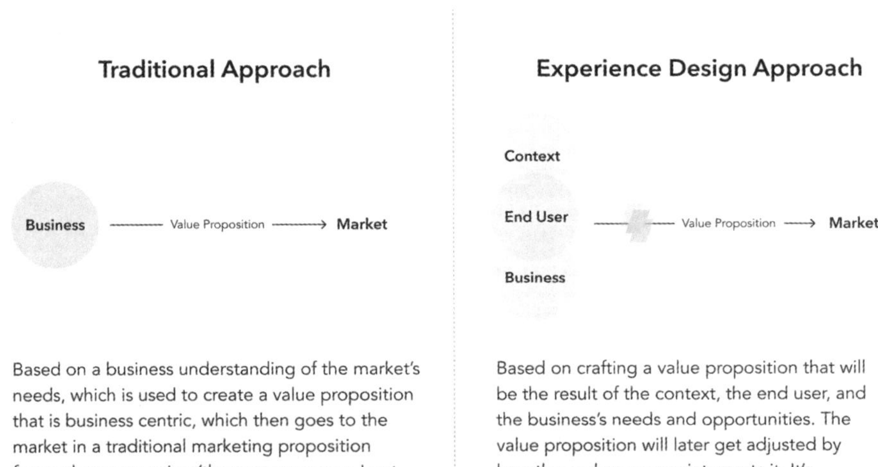

Reinterpreting Business Assets

The second fundamental is to truly understand and reevaluate your assets. These are not just the building or the machinery or the computer equipment. You have to ask yourself: How can I make my assets more scalable? When you view your assets through the lens of scalability, you realize that your real assets are not in brick and mortar or even the equipment you own; they are the data you collect and the insights they hold.

For example, say you have a supermarket with twenty stores and ten thousand shoppers going through every month. There are twenty thousand transactions and two million to five million goods being purchased. Once you have this data, you can now start analyzing it to understand and find patterns in the purchase behavior.

Your biggest asset is not the physical space of the shop; it's your ability to understand what's going on, what time your customers go shopping, what they buy, which products they buy together, which products they don't buy together, which offers work, and which don't.

This analysis shows you that your customers are mainly shopping after work, which creates inefficiencies due to large numbers of shoppers and an increase in queue length and wait time. During these times, you need to increase your physical capacity to accommodate this peak in demand. What are your options?

In essence, you can either "punish" the shoppers coming in at those peak times by increasing prices and delivering poor service. Or you can reward a change in behavior, perhaps offering discounts to those who visit the store during quieter times instead of after work.

Alternatively, you can transform. For example, you might say, "Look online while you're at work. Since we know what you bought the last ten times you visited the store, why not just click here, and we'll get your shopping ready and deliver it to your office or your home. Here's your order based on the items that you buy most often." That's transformation.

Agility and Speed

The third fundamental change is that speed is important. It's much more rewarding to put something quick and dirty into the market—the minimum viable product—than to wait until it's good and solid.

If you have an iPhone, every time you update it with the new iOS and it doesn't work or drains your battery, you hate it. But then, Apple sends a fix so you can go on using it. Everyone knows that something new is going to fade. No problem, because it generates not the expectation of perfection but the expectation of continuous improvement.

The disruptors are always spinning new ideas, creating something fresh, and for the customer, that's fine. Sometimes, the update doesn't work, but the customer expects you to fix it—and fix it quickly, within the next week or so. On the flip side, with traditional companies, the expectation is to do upgrades or updates once a year. That means you'd better get it right if your customer has to wait another year before any glitch is repaired—assuming they're prepared to wait and haven't already switched suppliers!

Horizontal Focus

The fourth fundamental is horizontal versus vertical integration—choosing to horizontalize your business and become a platform. You can achieve this by connecting your end users, whom you have an extensive profile about and a good relationship with, to the hundreds of suppliers that want to reach them.

Now, you've gone from a traditional vertical integration, where you would go up or down the supply chain, to a horizontal integration, where you're actually partnering with other non-associated businesses. All of this is to improve the experience of your asset, which is your customer, and to drive your business.

Leapfrog Regulation

Regulation is always late. There's always a time lag between innovation and regulation catching up. Something to keep in mind is, usually, the people who are responsible for developing the regulations behave and think like end users rather than like regulators.

For instance, we had a situation in Chile when the last season of *Game of Thrones* came out. Everyone on the planet was trying to watch it, and the internet connection dropped out because of this demand. Twitter was awash with people complaining that they paid for five hundred gigabytes but were getting nowhere near that. This created a lot of frustration, which continuously piled up.

To avoid this type of thing happening in the future, the regulators decided to constitute a law relating to minimum speeds. Thinking like an end user, the regulators felt that by ensuring everyone had to have a minimum internet speed, that would resolve the problem. But the internet is like a pipe; it depends on the demand being placed on it. If you go on at 3:00 a.m., you'll get five hundred or six hundred megabytes. If you go on at 9:00 p.m. when everyone is watching Netflix, then it's going to go down.

When you have a regulation that stipulates a minimum speed, it creates two effects. One, the telecom companies can no longer offer high speeds; they have to cap it in order to provide the minimum. Two, it stops the telecom companies from being disruptors. Instead of focusing on their customer and how they can ensure, based on their need and usage, each individual user reaches the minimum, their focus is turned inward, concentrating on how they can comply with the regulation.

In reality, the minimum speed actually relates to cable speed, and that means the speed to the socket. Notably, 99.95 percent of households use Wi-Fi connectivity. In this case, the speed depends on the thickness of your walls, the height of your roof, how much furniture you have, and where you put the router. It will even depend on the setup of your router. The majority of problems (85 percent) people have with the internet relate to the Wi-Fi router, not the Wi-Fi getting to the house.

So say a customer calls the telecom company complying with the minimum speed rule, asking for help with their internet connection. The company checks their logs and says, "Sorry—according to my system, you are getting the minimum speed of 500MB to your house. What you need to do is investigate the router. I can't help you with that because if I did, I could be liable." This is an example of bad regulation that drives behavior, leading to poor service.

Conversely, an example of good regulation is when it allows innovation and disruption. This is illustrated by the electric companies in Spain. The traditional model is that one electric company actually produces the electricity, one does the transmission, and one distributes it, the latter being the one that you pay the bill to. The others you don't really see.

Spain has deregulated the industry, meaning that I can be an electric company without actually owning or producing any electricity. I can just go to the market and buy electricity to sell. Now, because of the deregulation, there are suddenly a lot of disruptors coming into the market with a completely different approach. The electricity costs quite a lot of money, and most companies are actually losing money every time they sell a kilowatt, so what they do is try to help the customer save money by saving electricity.

The way they do that is by using data, artificial intelligence, and monitoring tools. This is how they work: They say, "You're going to pay the minimum kilowatt price in this country. We have different plans that you can select from, and according to that, we're going to give you a base rate. On top of that, if you want to save, we're going to assign an agent to you who will analyze your usage every month and make recommendations about how to save money and electricity. This is going to cost you a dollar and fifty cents extra per month."

Taking it even further, the electric company may continue with: "Also, we notice you have air conditioning. If you put an intelligent device on your air-conditioning unit, we can help you save up to 45 percent off your bill. We can also do the same thing with your heaters or any other appliance. We're going to get to know you and your home environment and provide these appliance monitoring devices at a cost of five dollars per month."

Now, the electric company has created engagement—because let's face it: Nobody likes dealing with electricity bills.

They might also say, "You have a smart meter and can see how much electricity you've consumed over the day—when you turned on the dishwasher or the washing machine or when you turned off the lights. It can be fun to keep checking and working out how to reduce your consumption and how much you're saving."

Now the customer is having an experience, and the company's product—electricity—becomes a service. They're renting out assets to help customers monitor their usage and save money on their electricity bill. They've started building a relationship with their customer rather than simply having a transactional interaction. From a business perspective, we're able to take this relationship of recurring business and use it as the basis for loans and growth.

So, to recap, bad regulation constrains the market, stops transformation, and stops disruption. Good regulation or the relaxation of regulation allows the market to flourish.

Turning a Transactional Interaction Into a Relationship—An Example

The final fundamental of experience-based businesses is to move from a transactional interaction to a relationship. For example, say a distribution company buys large quantities of goods at a cheap price and sells them to their clients—small local shops—in smaller quantities but at a higher price. Their clients then stock their shops with the products and sell them to their customers (the end users), again in smaller quantities and at a markup. The small shops buying from the distributor earn loyalty points based on their purchases, and once they've reached a certain level of points, they get a reward.

When starting out, this works well. The distributor's clients are satisfied with the loyalty points scheme and subsequent reward. However, over time, the small shops realize they don't actually want the rewards that are being offered, as they have other more important issues that are affecting their business.

The first problem is that they really want credit. If they can get credit from the distributor, then they can grow their business, and if they grow their business, then they can buy more from the distributor. The second problem is stock holding and replenishment. Since ordering is only done when the distributor's sales rep physically comes to the shop, that is their only opportunity to order. These visits are infrequent, so either the shop has to buy large quantities of stock, which they can't do because they don't have any credit facility, or they end up running out of products.

Once you understand some of the problems facing the client—in this case, the small shops—you can focus on traditional digitalization to address them—for example, automating the whole process by allowing online ordering and delivery. This is a definite improvement and does address at least one of their concerns: reducing stock holding while keeping products available. However, it misses the opportunity to change the game completely. Once you understand the motivations of the customer—to get access to credit and ensure availability without increasing stock holding—you can begin to transform the whole process.

To solve the stock and availability problem, the distributor could give their clients an app. The client could use that to take a picture of the product on the shelves, which gives the distributor an indication of their current stock levels and also shows how well the product is being displayed and marketed. Not only does this allow for automatic replenishment if stock levels are low, but it also allows for the distributor to reward the client with points if their marketing of the product is good.

However, perhaps the client doesn't have the right phone, which means they can't download the app, and the whole system fails. Except when we look at it as an opportunity for digital transformation, we realize the distributor can solve this problem for their client by offering to provide them with a phone on a permanent lease basis at five dollars per month.

When examining the issue of credit, the distributor may realize they don't actually want to get into lending money to these small shops. The solution: bring on board a bank to provide microcredits for their clients. By capturing the value of the transactions, they can earn commission on every microcredit provided.

Now, not only has the distributor reinvented themselves by leveraging their biggest asset—the relationship they have with our client—they have also evolved their business model using data and improved their client's experience in the process by understanding and addressing their problems. This distributor has transformed into a platform business!

Transforming Organizations Through Design

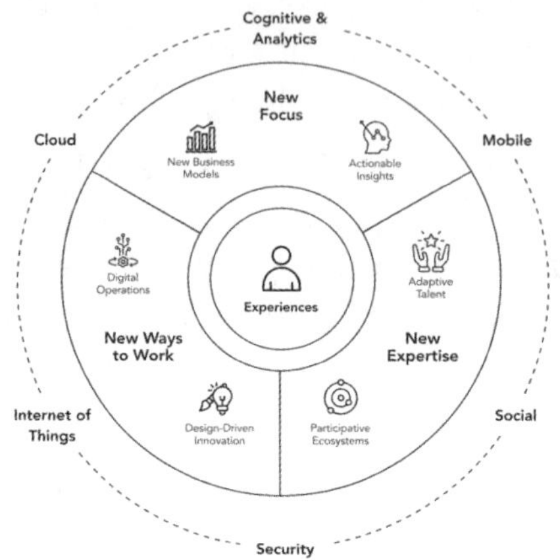

Unyielding customer experience focus through **digital transformation**

Transformation requires new capabilities. In essence, in order to transform as an organization, you need to explore the core business and the opportunity to reinvent or reimagine it. You also need to research, anticipate, and encourage the chance to do something new.

The focus is on continuous evolution because, otherwise, you're following the trend of disruption instead of setting it. In other words, you're just trying to keep up. It's about anticipating what your customer is going to want or need or what will meet their expectations.

Disruptors have not only changed the business model, but they have also changed how people work and engage with technology. Even my grandma uses Uber; she just taps on the app, and that's the simplicity that technology is allowing us to have today.

This changes the user's expectations. It's different from you selling something, putting it out to the market, and creating a need. Now, you're selling an experience, no matter the product, service, or industry. If you're in the coffee business, you're no longer selling the coffee bean or the latte. You're selling the experience created when the customer engages with you.

The next question is this: How do we create these experiences? By exploring technology and new business models, using predictive modeling, and defining experience:

- What technology and new business models are available that interconnect with your CRM and link to social media?
- How can you use predictive modeling? To follow the coffee analogy, you have the Starbucks app and are a block away from your local store. When you get a message asking if you want your regular latte, you click yes. Now, the preparation supply chain kicks into action, working out how long you're going to be and getting your latte ready so that when you arrive at the store, you walk in, pick up your coffee, use contactless payment, and continue on your way.
- What is an experience? It's about understanding not only your customer but also their needs and the relationship you have with them. It's likely you already have all this data, but it's just not being used in a way to create predictive models and real-time offers.

  For instance, every year, I book plane tickets for my entire family to go to Spain. If I book with an airline, each time, I have to go to their website, type in all my details, and get the standard price. If I use Expedia, they have my profile and annual requirements. Furthermore, they use that information to create a predictive model of when I am next likely to need plane tickets, and they send me a real-time offer for them. That means all I need to do is click on a button, and the tickets are purchased.

The goal is to drive impulsive behavior. It's about anticipating what a customer is likely to need and providing it without them having to do anything except pay. Even then, the organization probably has the customer's card details, so they just need to confirm that the card number is correct. This prompts on-the-spot consumption.

Example—Transforming the Customer Experiences as a Response to COVID-19

The Impacts of the COVID-19 Crisis Span Different Dimensions and Different Industries

Impact on Financial Markets

- → Institutional investors
- → Private investors
- → International security
- → Development financing
- → Financial and monetary systems
- → Geo-economics
- → Infrastructure
- → Automotive industry

Impact on Trade

- → Development financing
- → Financial and monetary systems
- → Geo-economics
- → Infrastructure
- → Automotive industry
- → Banking and capital markets
- → International trade and investments

Impact on the Workforce

- → Public finance and social protection
- → Future of economic progress
- → Corporate governance
- → Workforce and employment
- → Future of health and healthcare
- → Agile governance
- → Digital economy and society
- → Aviation, travel, and tourism
- → Supply chain and transportation
- → Retail, consumer goods, and lifestyle
- → Advanced manufacturing and production

- One of the major impacts of the COVID-19 crisis is focused on the **employability** and **use** of the **workforce** within companies.
- The crisis is leading governments, industries, and consumers to **reinvent the way** they **interact** with each other in accordance with **changes in consumption patterns** and **user needs**.

When COVID-19 hit, some of the first businesses to close were gyms. The majority decided to just shut down and cut their losses by firing employees and selling equipment. However, one gym decided to start working with me to see if they could find a way to keep their business going.

My initial assertion was that this was a great opportunity for digital transformation. We started by considering the assets of the company. In the traditional sense, we would normally think of the gym's assets as the equipment and machines. But when we reinterpreted them, we realized that the gym's biggest asset was the relationships between the trainers and the gym members. If the gym fired those trainers, it would lose its biggest asset, and then there would be zero opportunity to reinvent itself.

The next challenge was to ensure that the gym members who had paid their annual subscriptions were getting something for their money. To do this, we moved the gym classes onto Zoom. This was sufficient as a short-term solution, but soon, members were dissatisfied with these online classes, as they didn't always fit around their schedule, and they didn't feel they were getting value for money.

The next move was to provide more personalization. By increasing the number of classes, the times, and the availability, the gym was successfully running its business through digitalization. However, some of the classes, like spin, required equipment, and most people didn't have a spin machine in their homes. But there were fifty or so machines that sat in the gym not being used. The traditional view would be to sell them to realize their asset value. But when you look at this as an opportunity for transformation, you realize you can use the machines to provide a service.

The members were paying twenty dollars per month for the online classes, but if they paid an additional five dollars each month, the gym would deliver to their home a spinning machine, which they could rent permanently. Within a week, the entire gym was empty because even the weights had been rented out. Now, this business started sourcing the best equipment and getting it into the homes of their members as part of their service provision.

However, it became clear that some members were looking to cancel their membership because, despite attending classes, they were gaining weight. Although they were doing some exercise, being at home on lockdown and not eating healthily meant that the weight was piling back on.

Acting as a platform, the business decided to start delivering healthy food to their members. Partnering with a company that provided food boxes, they were able to offer members several options costing different monthly amounts as part of the same distribution method. The gym had successfully reinvented its business through three important principles:

- Viewing the customer, not the equipment, as the asset.
- Establishing a payment method (monthly subscription) that allowed the gym to offer additional services that customers could easily sign up for.
- Using data to understand what their customers' concerns, issues, and problems were.

There's never been a better moment to innovate and evolve. What the pandemic has created is this notion of permanent crisis. As businesses, we need to manage instability and anticipate changes.

Often, when businesses gain momentum and get bigger and bigger, it's like sailing a large ocean liner. A course is set, and the ship keeps going relentlessly on that course without deviation. There's so much inertia that even if you wanted to turn, so you cut the engines and applied the brakes, the ship would keep moving forward with a huge time lag before it would start to slowly veer from its original direction of travel. Businesses must realize that they need to navigate, not just follow a course.

Traditionally, a business sets its objectives, and the customer, product, or service becomes a consequence rather than a driver of those objectives. The COVID-19 crisis has caused us to move from static planning, where we plan once a year and then execute, to continuous planning, where we adjust based on execution and evolution. In other words, it has made us start operating in scenarios. Activating scenarios implies a process where we set a vision and then craft different routes to reach it, which is exactly how we strategize when we are designing experiences.

Imagine an annual report that says next year, we will have five different scenarios, and these are the probabilities of them happening. If this happens, we'll do this, and if that happens, we'll do that. Now, the business has used design to produce five varying strategies or directions of travel based on the possible environment they find themselves operating in.

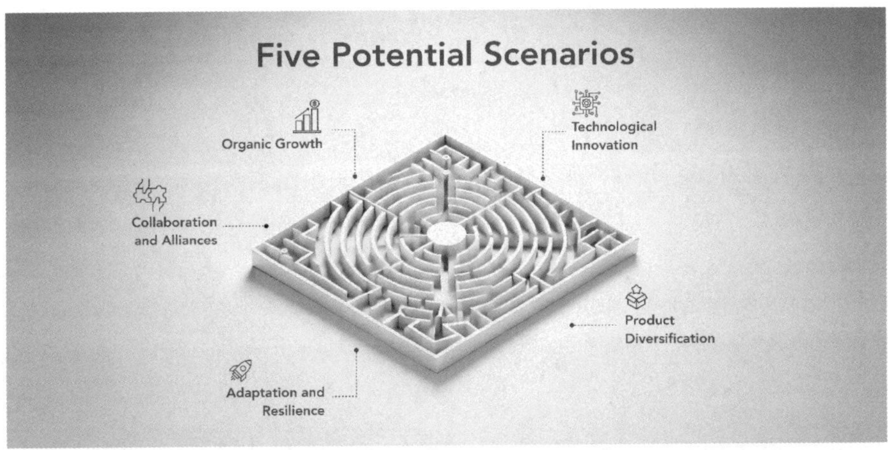

The key take-home message is this: When it comes to attracting and retaining customers, the experience is everything. That has to be at the center of every business action and decision.

After reading this chapter, you should have homed in on these key learning points:

- How to shift from being product centric to being customer centric.

- The importance of making your design so clear that it doesn't require explanation. It's intuitive!
- How design can be leveraged to offer customers the ease, safety, and freedom they are seeking.
- The role of innovation in crafting positive customer experiences.
- The fundamentals of experience-based businesses.

In the next chapter, we will put this knowledge into practice by exploring my framework for delivering business transformation through design. Let's continue!

CHAPTER 4

DELIVERING TRANSFORMATION THROUGH DESIGN

> *"Design is devising courses of action aimed at changing existing situations into preferred ones."*
>
> —Herbert Simon, 1996,
> The Sciences of the Artificial

How can we help people and businesses transform using digital strategies? As discussed in chapter one, the first wave of digital transformation involved the digitization of systems, processes, and forms. This second wave of digital transformation is where the true transformation takes place, and it starts with a choice about your route to digital [r]evolution.

You need to decide whether to evolve your core business by reimagining your current offer or to follow the path of disruption by exploring the opportunities for revolution within your business. To clarify, when we talk about digital [r]evolution, we are talking about the ability or the opportunity for an organization to evolve, which is **digital transformation,** or create something new, which is **digital disruption**.

Digital [R]evolution

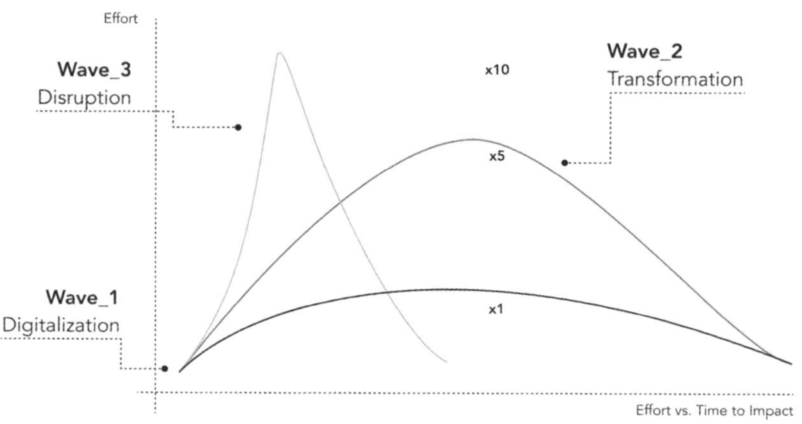

In this book, we're focusing on digital transformation through business evolution, which is a combination of strategy, creativity, innovation, and technology. It implies an evolution of your business DNA—a move from a transactional interaction with your customer to a relationship built on experience and empowerment.

A Word of Caution

In order to create digital [r]evolution, you first need to be able to detach. You must be prepared to abandon some of the things that currently make you, as a company, successful—to ditch some of the current practices and ways of operating and really be willing, able, and open to reinventing your business to create unique experiences.

I love the example of John Legere pictured below.

John Legere was an executive of AT&T in the US (left image) and then became the CEO of T-Mobile (right image). He decided to completely reinvent the experience and business model and how T-Mobile was using data. He wanted to challenge the key principle of how telecom companies have built their value proposition and their relationship with the customer.

But to do so, he needed to detach and reinvent himself first. Hence the transformation from a very classy and professional-looking executive in the first image to a more, dare I say, hip and trendy digital leader in the second! He wanted to create a whole new value proposition that encapsulated this way of rethinking the business model—elements such as "The customer has a plan, and it's very difficult to change it" and "If you don't use all your minutes or megabytes, you lose them." But first, he had to rethink (or perhaps redesign) himself!

Your choice will determine the level of transformation and the level of value that you can create. It's very important that you make a decision—you need to start somewhere, and you cannot start by doing both digital transformation and digital disruption at the same time.

The danger for organizations going down the disruption route before they've been through the transformation process is that they can get caught in what we call **corporate gravitational pull**. They start with the desire to be a disruptor, but as the disruption takes off, they bring it into their core business, killing the disruption and reducing the speed of transformation.

If you're a brick-and-mortar store, or if you aren't already a 100 percent digital company, don't try to be a digital company. Focus on understanding your DNA and reunderstanding your assets. From there, you can evolve your business model.

Remember, technology is just an enabler; digital transformation is about more than using the latest tech. True digital transformation is creating a new relationship with your clients and collaborators based on experiences, facilitated by a new or evolving business model and powered by data. You're looking for an evolution that will transform the value proposition, the customer experience, the business model, and the way you're using data and technology.

New Ways of Maintaining a Relationship

From Experience to Empowering

The Transaction Age			The Relationship Age
Data	Information	Knowledge	Insight
Product	Solution	Experience	Empowerment
Competition	Cooperation	Collaboration	Mutualism

Digital Technologies Are the Enablers of Transformation

Digital transformation is about reinventing the experience of your customers and collaborators to put a strong focus on the deep understanding of the customer. From this, you must create a new experience while also reinventing the relationship that the collaborator has with the company. It's about the opportunity to transform or evolve your business model, and this transformation or evolution is done from your current base.

Consider this: At this moment in time, what is the source of your organization's revenue? How can you start to evolve that business model? You need to begin thinking outside the box. In other words, let's forget what you've been doing for the last twenty to thirty years and reevaluate. What's the most important asset you have, and how can you use the data that you currently collect as a fundamental enabler for the transformation of your business?

For a long time, businesses have operated branches or retail units—activities that, in most cases, add very little value to customers and to the organization. The pandemic has broken down some of these cultural barriers and forced us to reconsider how we manage the activities we spend our time on. Ask yourself: How do I prioritize these activities? How do I use these branches or these interactions with the customer to move from a transactional relationship and engage in conversations about their future? How can I advise, help, or support them?

When you simply digitalize your processes, the digital world mirrors the physical world in terms of function, which makes little sense. When the customer goes into a store, they want different things from what they find in the digital world. So now it's a question of working out what interactions need to remain in the physical world and how you are going to add more value to this interaction.

One of the biggest problems we have in e-commerce is that we're faced with a website, a digital interface, that is not able to give advice or a recommendation. For example, say I want to buy a pair of running shoes. I know I have a certain foot shape, but it's very difficult to find an online retailer who is able to advise me on that. So I solve that problem by going to a store and asking for their recommendation.

When shopping online, you often get long and incomplete product descriptions, and you end up making a purchase based on aesthetics or price rather than what will meet your specialized need. We must recover that interaction and add value to it. Although there are chatbots available, they use an auto-response script based on your answers to set questions; they are not artificial intelligence able to help and guide customers as individuals. Above all, we have removed the human aspect that is able to understand, empathize, and recommend, which is one of the most important parts of the customer journey.

How are you going to complement the physical part with the digital part? One way is to take your salespeople and move them from a sales model to an advisor model, putting them on an online platform like Instagram or Facebook where they can interact on a one-to-one basis with customers looking for advice.

The next decision is this: What aspects of your online design will involve digitally interacting with human beings, and what aspects are you going to automate? Based on all these elements, how do you design this experience?

First, you examine your resources and perhaps decide to retain your sales force, but you have to give them some different tools. Implementing technology is always the final part of the solution to designing customer interactions, not the starting point.

This is the difference between a transformative process and a digitalization process. When you concentrate on digitalization, the focus is primarily on efficiency and improving customer service. See, by digitalizing components of a customer journey effectively, you are saving costs and therefore making improvements directly to your bottom line.

For instance, imagine you digitalize the checkout and payment process of a supermarket by swapping the cashiers for automatic checkout machines. You haven't transformed the process at all—the process is still the same: scan products and then pay for the total bill. However, you have reduced your overhead by introducing technology and a self-service model. While this digitalization of the process will require an initial investment, it will deliver savings on the running costs, which is why digitalization is so tempting for any organization.

However, as organizations implement digitalization processes in order to reduce costs, they risk affecting the overall experience of their customers and even of their own collaborators (employees). This is why it is so important to have a strong vision of the customer journey and customer experience—to ensure the digitalization efforts do not compromise that vision. The idea is to avoid falling into the trap of falsely believing digitalization is strictly making improvements when it might be negatively affecting the experience to the overall detriment of the organization.

Design is the key driver of digital reinvention. Just ask yourself a few simple questions: Would you be using Uber if the interface was bulky and complicated? Would you be using Airbnb if the site, and later the app, was dated and feature focused? Would you be shopping online with a complicated product listing-based website design?

Design is critical for brand adoption and brand stickiness. It drives not only our utilization and interaction with products and services but also the entire relationship we have with them outside their functional intent. We "perceive" a brand based on how it gets activated across its multiple channels. This perception becomes internalized as a feeling and manifests into a memorable experience only once it is consumed through an integrated digital and physical continuum, with the former serving to perpetuate the experience ubiquitously.

Business Purpose Is the Key to Extending the Experience

The evolution in consumer expectations, along with consumer behaviors, has created enormous pressure on organizations to do more than "just business." Customers today expect that the companies they use have a purpose, one that goes beyond making money and extends to a cause that benefits mankind. As such, we see companies pursuing a new set of values and goals, aligning themselves with causes that rally people around them. Supporting everything from bringing water to Africa to gender equality, companies are now on the verge of finding a sense of purpose they can navigate alongside their business values and goals.

When it comes to digital services, the design relationship with a brand is even more dominant than the physical interactions. Nowadays, we extensively use digital services in our daily lives—from messaging our friends to consuming the latest series to shopping for our groceries while on the go. Digital services have changed how we relate to people, places, companies, and brands.

Today, our digital experience expectations are never ending, and they continually rise as our favorite apps or digital services get updated on a biweekly basis. Governing this relationship is the design of the experience, which manifests as the design of a customer journey and of the product or service we consume. So, it's evident that companies need to pay critical attention to design. We demand more, and we expect more from our digital providers.

However, if we examine our relationships with our traditional service providers, we see that they have stayed virtually unchanged. Think about your last interaction with the local taxi service or the travel agency just around the corner from where you live. Besides the advances in technology and the changes in our behaviors as users, which have been accelerated over the last five years, we continue to use almost the same channels to deal with our traditional service providers.

Furthermore, the expectations we set for our digital interactions with these traditional service providers are far below the expectations we set for our new service providers. Is this good news for the traditional players? Of course not! We set a lower expectation because we label them as "legacy." Their brands no longer appear as innovative or edgy, and most importantly, they become less relevant in our daily lives. We place them in the commodity box, and our relationship moves from an experiential one to a purely transactional one.

But why? Why can't the digital interactions with our utility company, telecom provider, financial institution, airline, or government entity provide the same experience as when we interact with disruptors like Uber, Facebook, and Expedia? Why can't those digital interactions be as simple and pristine as the newcomers? The technology, fundamentals, and building tools are the same for both newcomers and traditional service providers. So why these radically different outcomes?

The difference lies in the approach. Digital disruptors start from scratch with a single relentless focus on a continual state of digital reinvention of their customers' experience. Conversely, traditional service providers focus on digitalizing their physical experience through mere process automation. Under this approach, companies do not transform or evolve due to the failure of reengineering the required customer experience journey to new technology realities.

Instead, islands of scattered new digital initiatives arise. These build new channels of interaction with customers, but they are still mostly based on traditional processes. Then, the scattered initiatives are measured with the same focus and KPIs as their traditional counterparts. Failing to demonstrate relevant traction, most of them are either abandoned or remain as a separate component of the organization, thus creating multi-gear organizations where the physical/traditional components strain the ability of the new initiative to provide a better customer experience.

The path toward a reinvented customer experience, which can lead to increased relevance and appeal to your customer, requires the company to reinvent itself. This is where digital reinvention comes into play, with design as the key component to drive evolution.

By putting design at the center of the reinvention, a company starts by envisioning and designing a new customer experience, then moves into articulating and executing this vision. This is not about moving physical interactions into a digital channel. It is about reimagining the relationship your company can have with a customer that is powered and boosted by digital technologies, which then are conveyed through people and process reinvention.

Companies aiming to regain "relevance" with their customers must reinvent their relationship with them. This relationship needs to embrace company roots and core services but can be augmented and enhanced using digital technologies. At the center of this reinvention sits design as the driving force. This can help a company envision this new relationship and then turn it into a consumable and actionable artifact.

Designing Your Business Transformation

There are three key strategies that I use with the organizations I work with to help them transform. These are the ingredients in your business transformation cocktail:

1. Create experiences.
2. Take care of the relationship throughout the entire customer life cycle.
3. Leverage specific drivers to define new solutions—what I call your backpack of solutions.

Creating Experiences—How Do We Design?

Interactive Holistic Simple

To begin, we look at needs. Design must fulfill a need wisely by focusing on your client and solving their problems. Remember, design starts and finishes with customers. It also must be proved through real experience. In other words, it must work (and be seen to work) in the real world. Finally, design is a holistic exercise around an experience, and it must be based on a simple and clear value proposition.

First, we need to truly understand the needs of the customer and solve their problems.

Second, we need to move from being brand or company centric to being user centric. In other words, we must consider what best serves the customer, asking how that fits with the company/brand.

Third, we need to implement an iterative process to evolve the design. We must be prepared to make mistakes, adapt, and learn from how our users are interacting with our products/services. It's not about getting one interaction right; it's about getting the entire experience right because we're measuring experience, not customer service.

Last but not least, the focus is on simplicity. Building and creating a design experience is about taking the simplest way. This means that creating experiences requires:

- Having a keen sense of the problem you are aiming to solve.
- Being clear about the value proposition so that it doesn't need an explanation.
- Being so clear about the interaction we are aiming to generate that it's intuitive.

In essence, you are creating a design experience that is going to drive consumption and drive the interaction with the customer just by how simple it is.

Taking Care of the Relationship

This stage of the mix requires you to put effort into the following key areas:

- Building relationships with clients before they engage with you as a business.
- Creating a unique and memorable experience to differentiate you from the competition.
- Promoting and supporting users to share and relive their experiences.

The life cycle of our customer is conceived by three clear steps.

First, it's about **planning** where you will start building the relationship and when you will begin engaging. Remember that you're trying to build relationships, not transactions. You're trying to have audiences that you nurture, not clients. However, at some point, these can be converted into customers. It may be that many will simply continue to be an audience, and that's fine. What you're trying to do here is plant the seed to create this relationship.

The second step is the **experience**. Because of the experience the audience has with your company, they consume the product or service and become a customer.

The final step is **remembering**. The customer is now a promoter or an advocate for the brand (or possibly a detractor depending on their experience). A customer turned promoter can help you evolve and interact in a different manner—remember the term co-collaborator mentioned in chapter two?

We've established that our customer's behavior has evolved and now demands a balance between physical and digital interaction. The key is to focus on searching for and creating unique multichannel experiences for that customer. Omnichannel isn't always the solution!

Customers are looking for new ways of interacting. They are generally more demanding, impatient, and pragmatic, seeking simple and quick ways to purchase. But they also want mobility and to be taken care of by both physical and digital channels in the best possible way.

As you've learned, customers are searching for experiences that go beyond a transaction, and they are willing to exchange information in order to get that personalization. They are also making more conscious purchasing decisions and open to paying more for brands that demonstrate shared values. Plus, they are comfortable and familiar with constantly changing trends and a fast-fashion market. Collaborating with your audience, customers, and promoters allows you to identify these changing trends and exchange personalized information in the process.

We know that as customers' expectations and interactions start evolving, they become more demanding. Now, with a single click, they can compare your prices anywhere in the world.

Amazon has started opening physical stores, something that a few years ago they said they would never do. One of the reasons for this change is that consumers would go to a local retailer where they could have a real human interaction. Once there, they would take out their smartphone, open the Amazon app, and use the barcode scanning feature to compare the prices.

If the price was close, they would buy it immediately, getting that instant gratification of purchasing the product and taking it with them. If the price was a little bit different, but the service that was offered was good, they would still buy it. But if the service was bad and the price was high, they would make the decision to buy it on Amazon, go home, and wait for it.

For the sake of efficiency, Amazon is stepping into reducing the time of delivery but at the same time opening physical stores. This is truly omnichannel engagement.

Consumers seek out physical interactions only if they are going to be meaningful and of value. With that in mind, you need to focus on creating a unique and symbiotic channel experience for your customer.

I see so many companies obsessed with building omnichannel experiences when what they have to truly create is a symbiotic relationship between their channels. That way, the consumer can use the right channel, in the right manner. As the organization designing the experience, you can decide how you're going to use the channel.

This is so important. It's a big mistake to try to have all the channels delivering the same type of experience because the channels are different. Therefore, you need to deliver the experience that is catered to that challenge in that particular moment. And it's really important that you get it right when you start combining the physical and digital world. When a customer communicates with your brand and engages with your product or service, they want you to listen to them and be able to reply in an appropriate way.

Leveraging Specific Drivers to Define New Solutions

So far, we've considered the first two ingredients of the transformation cocktail—creating experiences and taking care of the relationship. Now, we need to utilize our backpack of solutions to define our transformation strategy. This backpack includes:

- Reevaluating the business model.
- Defining the playbook experience.
- Generating data and actionable insights.

- Promoting loyalty.
- Exploring platforms.
- Creating the WOW factor!

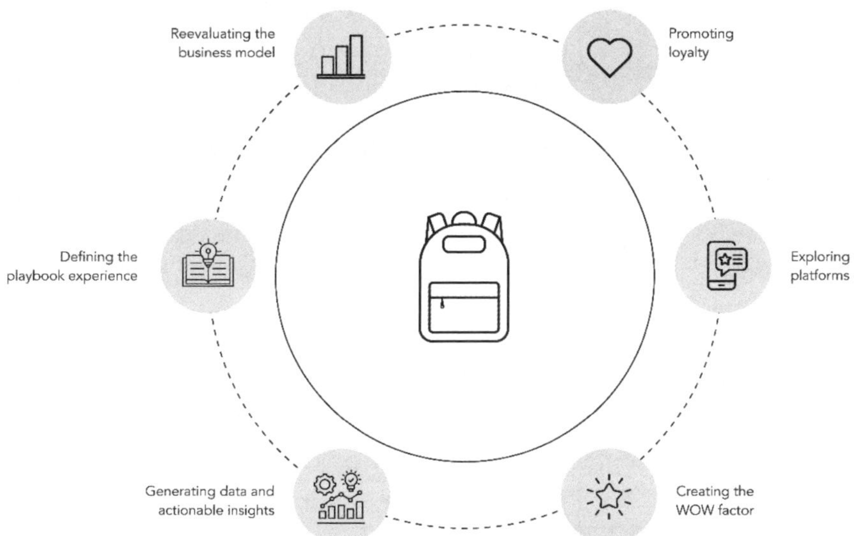

Reevaluating Your Business Model

This entails looking for and experimenting with new ways of generating income as well as building a relationship and interacting with the customer. It's about delivering a new experience through an enhanced or evolved business model that's based on a reunderstanding of data. Remember, a business model is really just a way of capturing and transforming value.

As an example, let's reevaluate the business model of a supermarket. The traditional grocery shop model is to buy goods, add basic value by displaying them so the customer can easily compare different brands, and then sell them. The profit is basically the margin—the difference between the price the store pays for the goods and the price it charges for them. If this particular supermarket decided it was time to evolve their business model, they could do it in a number of ways:

Bundling	Package related goods together (e.g., a main meal, dessert, and bottle of wine for a set price).
Freemium	Offer basic services such as using an app to place an online order for free—like click and collect—but then charge a fee for a premium service, which allows the customer to book a time slot for home delivery.
Discounting	Offer a high-margin product like an electric toothbrush below cost in order to drive sales of the low-margin toothbrush heads.
Reverse discounting	Offer the low-margin item (toothbrush heads) below cost to encourage purchase of the high-margin companion product (electric toothbrush).
Adding services	Offer financing to customers through a branded credit card. Because you're not a financial institution, you might move from paying your suppliers on the day you receive the goods to ninety days after, meaning you can now lend this money to your customers for ninety days, collecting all sorts of data on your customers' buying patterns as you go.

Subscription	Charge a fee to gain access to a service like having a personal shopper, discounts/special offers, or exclusive products.
Commodity purchasing	Add rapid purchase buttons to the app for products that individual shoppers buy in the same quantity every month, making purchasing easier and quicker and prompting purchase through reminder messages.
Become a destination	Build a community of customers who don't go to the store for commodities but to learn about ingredients, cooking, recipes, and samplings and attend specialized talks or meet and greets.
Pay as you go	Offer the opportunity for customers to turn up with their list and hand it to a personal shopper to collect while they go off for tea and cake in the café—all for a one-off fee.

These are just some of the possible evolutions of a supermarket's business model. There are others that may be more relevant to your business, brand, or industry:

Exclusivity	Pay royalties to another (perhaps larger) organization for the right to sell your product exclusively to their customers (e.g., employee reward schemes).

Brokering	Bring together buyers and sellers charging a fee per transaction (e.g., online auction sites).
Differential pricing	Charge different rates for different levels of service (e.g., mobile phone tariffs).
Crowdsourcing	Get a large group of people to contribute content for free in exchange for access to other people's content (e.g., TikTok, YouTube).
Leasing	Rent rather than sell high-priced products (e.g., cars).
Product to service	Rather than selling the product, sell the service the product performs (e.g., carpet cleaning).
User communities	Give members access to a network and content, charging for both membership fees and advertising (e.g., Angie's List)

Defining the Playbook Experience

This means defining the vision for your commercial partners and priority customers. Wherever you are in the world, you must craft the same experience for your customers.

It's like the Starbucks example: If you go into a Starbucks in the UK, Spain, Los Angeles, or China, you will see the same components and will have the same experience. The way to codify that experience is through a playbook.

Once you understand that you are operating in experiences, you understand that your experience needs to be recognizable, but you may need different flavors depending on your customer.

For example, it's going to be different if you are contacting British Airways over the phone, via Twitter/X, or at the actual desk in the airport. But all of them need to deliver a recognizable experience that is distinctly British Airways.

The mistake many companies make is considering each channel separately and using a different process depending on the channel. This creates inconsistency in managing your customer, potentially damaging your brand and your relationship with that customer.

Your playbook sets out how you're going to operate across all the different channels under the umbrella of experience. Again, with the example of Starbucks, they are focused on becoming your third place—not your home, not your office, but a third place where you experience coffee.

The moment you develop your playbook, you then start developing KPIs to track that experience. For Starbucks, that is not the number of coffees they sell or the number of customers going through their stores; it is the amount of time the customer spends in Starbucks. Why? Because the more time someone spends in store, the more likely they are to consume coffee or other products.

So the initial step is getting the customer to go into the store in the first place. The next step is creating an experience to ensure the customer wants to come back. This time, rather than taking their coffee to go, they'll drink it in store. Then, next time, they'll use the Wi-Fi to get up to date with emails and add a pastry or lunch to their coffee order.

The playbook experience is the same principle used by top sports teams who have set plays for different scenarios they encounter on the field. It's the idea of "In order to cause this to happen, we intend to do the following to change the behavior of the opposing team." It's no different for businesses. Remember the five possible annual report scenarios we mentioned in chapter three?

Generating Data and Actionable Insights

Project Title	Disruption
Project Lead	Ana
Client	InnovateTech Solutions

Project Overview	Goals and Objectives	The Problem
InnovateTech Solutions is a mid-sized tech company experiencing rapid growth and facing significant industry disruption. They are currently expanding their product line to include AI-driven solutions and need to ensure their data is effectively utilized.	The goal is to assess the current state of the company, identify areas for improvement, and align the business strategy with core values and objectives.	InnovateTech Solutions has been collecting a vast amount of data but lacks a unified approach to using it effectively. They also need to define their purpose beyond just business.
Brand Competitors	**Guidelines**	**Target Audience**
1. TechAdvance Inc. 2. AI Innovators 3. DataGen Solutions	Follow the brand guidelines provided in the initial client brief. These include using the company colors (blue and green), maintaining a professional and innovative tone, and ensuring all communications are customer centric.	Primarily B2B clients in the technology sector, focusing on mid to large-sized companies. Age range: 30–55. Geographical focus: North America and Europe.
Budget and Timeline	**Deliverables**	**Brand Messaging and Tone**
Budget: $50,000 Timeline: January to June 2025	A comprehensive report on the current state, a set of strategic recommendations, and an implementation plan.	InnovateTech's messaging should be aligned with their core values of innovation, customer centricity, and integrity.

This involves using both quantitative and qualitative data to identify actionable insights by leveraging new points of contact within the digital ecosystem. Data is something that all organizations have, but the crucial part is how you turn that data into something actionable.

Interestingly, as Raven, we did our own study of the top Latin American organizations and their use of data. One hundred percent of those companies insisted that they based everything they did around the customer, but less than 7 percent recognized that their offers were generic and not targeted based on the customers' needs or wants.

For instance, suppose you are a telecom customer, and you decide to leave your provider. When you tell the company you are leaving, they will generally offer you a discount or incentive to stay. Remember, this is a generic incentive that is offered to anybody considering leaving—perhaps 10 percent off your next bill. There is no attempt to understand the decision-making behind the desire to change providers.

What the company could do instead is use the information they already hold about you and try to understand who you are, what you care about, and therefore how they might be able to incentivize you to stay. It may not be money that is driving your move to another provider.

The other way to use data to drive actionable insights is by being preemptive. Perhaps a company notices that a customer hasn't used their credit card in the last four days, and normally they use it at Tesco every Tuesday when they go shopping. This indicates maybe they got a card with a different credit provider.

Or perhaps when you look at the data, it becomes obvious based on a customer's purchase history that they recently got married or had a baby. By looking at the data you already hold on your customers, you can understand the life events taking place and turn this insight into an action to create a better relationship with that customer. For instance, if the customer starts spending money on baby clothes, you could initiate a conversation about getting a new, more family-friendly car or perhaps buying a bigger house.

This type of analysis can be done on a group level as well as an individual level. By analyzing groups of customers, perhaps those who use their credit card regularly and those who only use it from time to time, you can make sure you're giving the people who are spending a lot of money on their card the right experience so they continue using it. For those who only use it occasionally, you can find out more about them and plug into what they really want in order to increase their spending.

At first glance, this type of data gathering can seem quite intrusive. But actually, we're already bombarded by generic marketing messages that are either irrelevant or have been triggered by a misinterpretation of your browser history or social media activity (the click ads approach). But if, as a customer, I feel understood because any offers you send me are relevant to my current situation and preempt a need I might have now or in the future, then that strengthens my relationship to your company.

The important point here is that you need to be able to profile your customer to offer personalized experiences to your target audience by understanding who they are and how they are connected to your value proposition.

Perhaps the first step all companies can take, and one that will immediately improve the experience of their existing customers, is to get all the data they hold on them—their name, address, ID number, email address, telephone number—in one place. This is all basic information that most businesses already possess, but how often when contacting a company do they ask you for information you know they already have? Your provider should already know your name, your email, where you live, etc. After all, they're charging you every single month for it!

So, as an organization, it's important to aggregate each customer's data and have it at your fingertips so that you don't have to rehash the same conversations with each customer interaction. That frees you up to focus more on resolving their challenges, adding additional value, and, of course, optimizing the customer's overall experience.

Promoting Loyalty

This is about finding a way to strengthen the relationship you have with your customer throughout the entire life cycle. When you think of promoting loyalty, reward schemes like Air Miles or Tesco points may come to mind. Many of these types of schemes were abandoned because they were just too expensive, especially for smaller businesses. But what technology has allowed us to do is turn loyalty schemes from an extra cost into a means of income generation.

Let me give you an example. An insurance company specializes in health insurance policies. In exchange for a fee, they give you a health insurance policy and an Apple Watch. If you walk ten thousand steps every day, they reduce the cost of your policy by 20 percent.

So now you're engaged as a customer because you want to remain healthy and know that ten thousand steps a day will help with that. But in addition, you'll be getting a benefit in your bank balance. It becomes like a computer game—you get in your steps and claim your reward.

The insurance company has changed their business model—they're no longer selling health insurance; they're helping their customers live healthier lives. They've created a playbook experience and a mutually beneficial relationship where both sides get something positive from the interaction.

Now, your customer becomes a promoter because their friends and family want in too. Not only that, but they want to be able to compete against each other in terms of how many steps they've taken each day. That's good for the insurance company because there are fewer payouts and good for the customer because they are fitter, healthier, and seeing the benefit in reduced premiums.

However, the insurance company goes one step further. Using data analytics, they notice that on the renewal form, the customer has said that they go to the gym regularly. The company approaches the gym owners and agrees that whenever one of their policyholders uses their gym, they will pay them one dollar. The gym now has an incentive to encourage their current customers to take out health insurance policies and also to encourage those customers with policies to attend more regularly. It's a cost for the insurance company that is offset by an uptick in new customers as well as existing customers living a healthier life and therefore requiring less payouts.

A few months later, the health insurance company realizes they have been extremely successful in driving the behavior of their customers to exercise more and are now paying the gym owners two thousand dollars per month. Now, their business model can adapt again. Instead of paying the gym owners whenever their customers attend, they now have the leverage to say, "We're happy to recommend your gym, and in return, you pay us fifty cents every time they attend."

This example takes us nicely to the next solution in our backpack . . .

Exploring Platforms

This involves identifying new ways to connect, interact, and sell to partners and clients. In the health insurance example, the company recognized their playbook experience was about managing the experience of a healthier life for their clients and partnered with a gym to help achieve this.

Becoming a platform business requires you to reinterpret your assets. Once you reexamine them, you'll probably realize you have some that you haven't put enough effort into; instead, you've been putting your time and energy into assets that are less valuable.

Turn your attention from your physical assets—the buildings and equipment—and zero in on your clients and your relationships with them. Examine your touchpoints with the customer—for instance, the delivery driver who knows where they live and whether they're happy for the delivery to be left on their porch. You need to think about a new way of capturing value.

How does this information allow you to give your customer a better experience? How do you turn your business model from one that sells them a product or service to one that allows them to experience a better life?

WOW Factor

Finally, you need to consider the WOW factor by creating experiences that surprise your customers and generate moments of serendipity. After all we've covered so far, you probably aren't surprised to discover it is actionable insights driven by data that deliver the WOW factor.

Imagine you've just arrived at Emirates airlines. You take a seat, and before you know it, they bring you your favorite drink, which just happens to be a ginger ale without ice. How do they know that? Because the last five times you traveled with Emirates airlines, you put a ginger ale without ice on your account. So this time, it was all prepared and ready for you.

That moment of serendipity is something unexpected that really blows you away because you didn't know they knew you so well. You didn't even know that they were interested in knowing you that well! This is no longer a transaction where you buy travel from them and they transport you to your destination. This is a relationship that has engaged with you, that values you as an individual, and that "gets you" as a customer.

It's the sort of experience you might get from your favorite B&B. Say every year you book a long weekend at a particular

B&B. You love the area, and the B&B owners are friendly and accommodating. But this year, you're surprised and delighted to find a bunch of daffodils in your room. These just happen to be your favorite flower!

It turns out that the owners remembered a conversation (data) from last year when you'd mentioned how much you like daffodils (actionable insight). They had written it down next to your customer details (your customer profile) so that the following year, they could surprise you with a bunch in your room (WOW factor).

Now, how likely is it that you'll book for next year? Perhaps even before the end of this year's stay! That's the WOW factor you're looking for—one that delivers an experience, builds a relationship, and generates loyalty. Remember, this does not happen by chance; it is DESIGNED!

The key take-home message is that digital strategies are essential for successfully transforming—and eventually disrupting—your business through design.

Now that you've made it to the end of this chapter, you should have a grasp on:

- The role of design and technology in instigating a digital [r]evolution.
- The steps of the customer life cycle and how to design customer experiences that develop an ongoing loyal relationship.
- The ingredients in your business transformation cocktail, including your backpack of specific drivers that are key to defining new solutions.

In the next chapter, I'll use case studies to demonstrate how successful companies have used these methods to evolve their businesses.

CHAPTER 5

CASE STUDIES

"Quality in a service or product is not what you put into in. It is what the customer gets out of it."

—Peter Drucker

The following case studies offer brief snapshots of how successful organizations are using the methodologies outlined in this book to transform the way they do business. Each case study starts with a look at what drove or inspired the need for change, then dives into what these companies do differently. Finally, the case study describes how they successfully transformed their business through design and how to achieve similar results in other industries/organizations.

Let's dive in!

Disclaimer: These case studies have been developed based on interviews and research using public information. They do not represent the views of the companies themselves.

STARBUCKS

To inspire and nurture the human spirit—one person, one cup, and one neighborhood at a time.

Industry	Retail/hospitality
Overview	Starbucks has over thirty-two thousand stores in eighty countries and is considered the premier roaster and retailer of specialty coffee in the world. Their aim is this: "With every cup, we strive to bring both our heritage and an exceptional experience to life."

What Inspired the Need for Change?

Starbucks opened its first store in 1971 in Seattle's Pike Place Market, offering some of the world's finest fresh-roasted whole bean coffees. By 1983, inspired by the romance of the coffee experience and the coffeehouse tradition in Italy, the vision of a third place between work and home was born. Starbucks wanted to be a different kind of company, one that not only celebrated coffee but that also provided a feeling of connection, a place for conversation, and a sense of community.

At the time, America was seeing a shift toward the fast-food culture, with business models focused on reducing costs while driving footfall and throughput in stores. Unfortunately, this was often at the expense of the quality of the product.

Starbucks decided to do things differently. They took the concept of "fast food," combined it with America's love of coffee, and decided to deliver an experience with the essence of an espresso from Italy. Ultimately, they created a new category of premium coffee, replacing traditional coffee machines and instant granules and bringing specialty coffee to daily life.

How Did They Successfully Transform Their Business?

What Starbucks did was codify a product that was not being consumed in the form it is today. At the start of its transformation, the majority of people drank instant coffee from granules. However, Starbucks took specialty coffee and turned it into an experience.

Customers can see the beans being ground, the coffee being made by the barista, and their names written on their individually prepared drink. They get to choose whether to take it away or sit in and enjoy the ambience. In essence, Starbucks created an experience beyond coffee.

From there, Starbucks started measuring its success not in terms of footfall through stores or numbers of coffees sold but by the amount of time customers spent in store. How did they change the fast-food behavior of the American public? They designed a welcoming atmosphere with comfortable seating and a familiar environment using lighting, layout, aromas, and music. Then, they expanded their offerings to include other drinks, snacks, and light meals. Today, wherever you are in the world, you can walk into a Starbucks store and know exactly what to expect.

Starbucks reinvented the functional and undifferentiated action of drinking coffee as an experience in which coffee became part of an overall brand proposition. When you go to Starbucks, it's not just to have a good coffee but to have a pleasant stay in a space with certain characteristics that allow you to live a desired experience. From the moment you enter, each contact point is thought out: where you stand in line alongside the pastry counter to tempt you with a piece of cake; the custom products, including mugs, that you can purchase; the attention and good spirits of the "partners"; and the favorable atmosphere to meet friends or work.

Starbucks invites its customers to be brand advocates. It offers them a simple experience that listens to their needs and builds loyalty through rewards programs so that they generate gratitude and trust with the brand. This shows us that design goes beyond basic aesthetics. It is about understanding the problems and needs of customers and encapsulating them in a journey with each of their interactions.

One of Starbucks's six principles is to develop enthusiastically satisfied customers all the time. From entering the store to finishing off the very last drop of coffee, it is a must that the customer feels the uniqueness of enjoying their Starbucks coffee experience.

How does the company know they are getting it right? Consider this: Starbucks has over twenty million regular customers each week and yet spends less than one percent of its annual revenue on advertising, relying instead on word-of-mouth recommendations. With all the elements in place that create an experience beyond coffee, it is possible to really feel welcome in this third place where people can gather and build a sense of community. And even if you go to Starbucks only to get a coffee, you are consuming a value proposition where coffee is not the center.

How to Achieve These Results in Other Businesses/ Industries

To move this value proposition from a product-centered one to a user-centered one, it is fundamental to look at your customers' needs and desires and to continually evolve, seize the moment, and keep pace with them. You need to recognize where the opportunity lies for the value proposition and develop a deep understanding of your consumer and the market opportunity.

In this case, Starbucks identified that Americans tended to drink a lot of coffee and also embraced a culture of fast food. But from their experience of roasting and selling specialty coffee beans, they also knew that once consumers were exposed to the superior quality of their product, they would be prepared to pay a premium.

Starbucks took this insight, combined it with an evolved fast-food café, and delivered an experience that their customers could engage with. In effect, they encouraged their customers to drink better coffee, to experiment with different types (cappuccino, latte, iced), and to interact with both the company and the community of Starbucks customers by sharing their experiences. This was then codified into an experience playbook that could be replicated in any store anywhere in the world.

The advantage of this approach is that the daily interaction and engagement with your customers means you can keep in touch with their evolving needs and use this to inform and update your value proposition.

Questions to Ask:

1. What is the experience you're delivering?
2. What insights about your product/service/market could be used to educate/inform/engage with your customers?

3. How can you better interact with your customers to ensure the evolution of your value proposition is in line with their changing needs?
4. How are you currently measuring success? How might your KPIs be changed to ensure the customer experience and value proposition are being evaluated?

APPLE

We believe that we are on the face of the earth to make great products and that's not changing.

Industry	Technology
Overview	Apple is a multinational corporation that creates consumer electronics, personal computers, servers, and computer software as well as distributes digital content. The company also has a chain of retail stores—Apple Stores—to showcase their core products: the iPhone smartphone, iPad tablet computer, and Macintosh computer line. It is the largest publicly traded corporation in the world by market capitalization with an estimated market capitalization of 2.81 trillion as of February 2024 and a worldwide annual revenue, which grew from 65 billion dollars in 2010 to 156 billion dollars in 2012.

What Drove or Inspired the Need for Change?

After three decades as predominantly a manufacturer of personal computers (Apple II, Macintosh, and Power Mac), Apple faced rocky sales and low market share during the 1990s. This prompted the return of Steve Jobs, who had been ousted in 1985 and was the starting point that transformed Apple into one of today's most admired brands.

With the company on the verge of bankruptcy, he installed a new corporate philosophy of recognizable products and simple design driven by the awareness that consumers were frustrated by how all the other technology brands designed their products in a lab without any thought for the end user. Jobs pushed Apple to start with the consumer experience and then work back to technology—"Apple makes technology so simple that everyone can be part of the future."

The next decade saw the launch of iTunes, the iPod, the iMac, the MacBook Pro, the MacBook Air, the iPhone, and the iPad. These products dramatically changed the company and turned Apple into one of the most valuable companies in the world.

How Did They Successfully Transform Their Business?

Nokia and Ericsson built better phones but were focused on the engineering and functionality. In the beginning, Apple wasn't able to produce a better phone, but it was able to create a better experience. However, at the time, nobody was thinking about experience.

When iTunes launched, everyone thought Apple was crazy to charge a dollar and ninety-nine cents per record when the current practice was to rip off MP3s onto CDs. Why would anyone buy something that they could get for free?

They did it because it was convenient. Apple had done something that, from our perspective now, was kind of obvious but at the time was not evident. It created synergy between the hardware, the physical component, and the software.

Most other companies were focusing on one or the other; for instance, Microsoft did software, and Compaq/HP did hardware.

This meant that specific hardware was configured to only run with certain software, and software was coded for specific types of hardware.

Apple removed this friction by adopting the concept of an open environment. It created an ecosystem, like a walled garden, that lives within a component—for example, the iPhone. Apple made it easier for developers and companies to enter the ecosystem and provided lots of tools for them to actually develop for that ecosystem.

Welcome to the App Store! Can you imagine your phone now without apps or an App Store? Previously there was no curation, no focus, no quality check, and no protection. With a closed ecosystem, Apple recognized the experience (and reassurance) provided by the ability to register your payment details on the app and pay for things using your phone rather than giving it out to various random companies. This paved the way for the evolution of the Apple Card. It's not a bank, but still, you're making payments through it. It's not a music store or retailer, but you still buy music through it.

Experience is at the heart of everything that Apple does, and that experience starts even before you consume the product. When you go to the store to purchase your Apple device, it's how the store manager approaches you, how the sales team behaves, the cleanliness of the tables, and the lack of clutter from cables. It's the fact that the team comes to you with a handheld card machine to process your payment. Then, it's getting the boxed product, taking it home, and unwrapping it. How many of us still have the empty Apple iPhone box at home in a drawer because we can't contemplate the thought of throwing it away? All this adds to the Apple experience.

Fundamentally, Apple is good at understanding human beings and using design to solve problems in an experiential way. It is not simply solving in a functional manner—rather, experience is front and center. It's all the extra details that make the difference. It's bigger than the product and what the customer sees or experiences; it's redesigning how the whole company operates. That's what generates the strong relationship between consumer and provider, and it's why Apple is able to charge a premium.

So, what did Apple get right? First, it removed the friction between hardware and software. Apple also made it easier for anyone to register (with a credit card) and create and upload software to the app store (without formal coding knowledge). By not making the apps proprietary, it increased the variety of features available to users and ensured users had access to the best apps, all on their Apple product. It brought in expertise, excellence, and innovation from outside the company, which enhanced the user experience. All in all, Apple created an ecosystem of easy-to-access, varied, and quality software all in one protected place.

Second, it put the customer at the center of its value proposition by starting with the consumer before the functionality of the product. This was embedded in the very DNA of the company from the CEO down.

Third, it created an experience that went beyond the essential use or consumption of the product. The priority was building a relationship and trust with the customer, an ongoing focus that allows Apple to sell more products. You know what you're going to get with an Apple product, be it an iPhone, an iPad, or an Apple Card. The brand relationship is so strong that even if Apple ventured into the transportation industry, you would likely trust them to sell you a car!

How to Achieve These Results in Other Businesses/ Industries

One of the most important learning points from the Apple case study is the value of the ecosystem. Companies tend to try to do everything by themselves. This was one of the failures of Nokia, which wanted to build the operating system, the phone, and the apps. It was the same with Microsoft and Windows.

Apple acknowledged that innovation would come from the ecosystem. Yes, the innovation arises in a wilder manner, but Apple set the rules and ensured some commonality for implementation, which allowed for easier access without the need for formal coding expertise. Thus, it sped up innovation.

A key driver of growth, value creation, and design is the need to understand the customer in a way that requires a more humble, more vulnerable approach. In other words, an approach that is not about you having all the answers and trying to fit them to the customer. Rather, it's about learning, understanding, acknowledging, and recognizing problems and using them to compose a new product.

This introduces the fundamental concept of market agility rather than market perfection. Many times, Apple has released an upgrade that didn't work, or the system crashed. No problem—they just fixed it. It was a screw-up, but it's part of the process—they fail fast, and they do it pretty well.

The other success was to reintegrate with retail. When Nokia, Samsung, and everyone else was closing retail stores and relying instead on telecom operators to sell their phones, Apple was doing the opposite. It took a completely different approach by introducing flagship stores, which enhanced the experience, created more of a relationship with the brand,

and became an iconic way to actually sell and position new products.

It's a constant evolution. Apple didn't stop; it applied the same principles to other industries and created disruption. Now, it's entering the games market and complementing the Apple Watch with a focus on health through Apple Health.

The organization has evolved from the early stages of simply selling computers to providing lifestyle solutions using subscription programs that accommodate the varying interests of its wide-ranging customers. Whoever you are, wherever you are, and whatever your interests, Apple is likely to have something for you. A large proportion of their customers may have five or six different subscriptions, including Apple iCloud, Apple TV, Apple Music, etc. And for each, you pay a subscription.

Being part of this Apple ecosystem means that for every evolution, the customer becomes more and more involved, and there is less likelihood of them exiting. They can get everything they want through Apple, which keeps building the experience.

The key takeaway is this: When you go to the Apple Store to purchase a new device, Apple isn't selling you a phone; it's selling you access to an ecosystem.

Questions to Ask:

1. How could your business benefit from placing an emphasis on building an ecosystem?
2. How would that ecosystem drive innovation, creativity, and a better relationship with your customers?
3. What new insights might be provided if you started with a focus on learning, understanding, acknowledging,

and recognizing the problems/issues/frictions of your customers?

4. How concerned are you about product perfection versus market agility?

DISNEY

Delivering the most exceptional entertainment experiences for people of all ages.

Industry	Entertainment
Overview	The Walt Disney Company is a global entertainment company operating theme parks, resorts, broadcast television networks, and digital content streaming services. With its theme parks, Disney has created an extremely loyal fan base, welcoming 157 million visitors in 2018 and boasting an incredible 70 percent return rate of first-time guests.

What Does Disney Do Differently?

From their first day at Disney, employees are clear that their primary purpose is to create happiness for their guests. With each interaction, they are encouraged to consider how they can use it to create magical moments and provide happy memories. This is prioritized above all else, so there is never a shortage of people looking to understand a guest's needs and find a way to help. If something goes wrong, every cast member knows it's their problem to fix, regardless of how it occurred in the first place or who was responsible.

It sounds fairly obvious, but the difference in Disney is that the company actually gives its employees the authority to solve the problem rather than go through layers of management for even the simplest solution. Many companies spend their time and effort getting customers to the point of sale, prioritizing marketing and engagement to encourage the initial purchase. After that, the level of service often drops. Disney understands that the real sale doesn't begin until after the initial purchase, and if they focus their efforts there, then future sales will take care of themselves. The value placed on the lifetime customer relationship is what drives the impressive 70 percent return rate for first-time visitors.

If we think about Disney today, we see multiple formats. The amusement parks are just an extension of its brand and experience, a way to create further relationships between Disney and its customers and to tell its stories at a different level.

Disney has been telling stories since its inception, but now, the story has become interactive. The theme parks promote active participation, and the guest is now part of the story.

Even queueing becomes part of the overall experience—in fact, it's integral, as it helps build the anticipation of the attraction to come. While in line, guests are talking and interacting with each other, scanning QR codes to get relevant updates, and posting on social media. If you completely reduce the queue to zero, then you lose the opportunity to create excitement about what happens next. Having to be patient and wait for the reward enhances the value of that experience.

Sure, the first thing that springs to mind when thinking about lines is that they're bad, but effectively managed queues generate excitement, anticipation, and interaction with other people who are also waiting. It becomes part of the overall enjoyment of the experience.

Disney invests a lot of money to achieve this using scenery relevant to each ride (e.g., Pirates of the Caribbean or Avatar) so guests are still getting the experience of the attraction before the main event. Far from being a point of friction, the queue can be an opportunity to upsell—food, drinks, merchandise—and can actually benefit the business.

In addition, Disney creates truly immersive experiences leveraging data. It uses more than fifteen thousand speakers and complex algorithms to play ambient music at a constant volume throughout the park. The Smellitzer machine was invented to pump scents through hidden vents so that the resorts always smell appealing. Main Street often smells of popcorn, and individual rides have their own unique scents, which adds to the overall ambience.

This highlights the fact that, as a business, you don't need to be in hospitality to think through the tiniest of details that enhance the customer's interaction and immersive experience. Even just changing the language from customer to guest puts the entire organization in service mode. When you're treating people as guests, you honor them, take care of them, and give them an experience. This is a totally different concept from thinking of them as customers in a transaction.

The other thing Disney has mastered is the idea of a playbook. You can go to Disney in different parts of the world and enjoy pretty much the same experience. You know what you're going to get. The same Mickey Mouse, the same fireworks—everything works seamlessly and doesn't get boring. It's comfortably familiar.

The cast members follow the playbook as a way to deliver a great experience. And now Disney is using digital technology to further transform its theme parks. Brightly colored trash cans are located around the parks within thirty feet of each other because research has shown that people will only walk thirty feet to throw something away. Sensors on the trash cans and in bathrooms monitor their use and send an alert when they need to be emptied. An underground network of pipes connects many of the trash cans and is programmed to empty them every twenty minutes. This attention to detail highlights how Disney is committed to removing anything that might hurt the experience, like an overflowing trash can.

The company also realizes that many of their guests are continually accessing data on the go, so it leverages technology through apps and mobile experiences. This includes free Wi-Fi throughout all the parks. Guests can get real-time information about ride wait times, park events, and hours through the My Disney Experience app, which even includes features such as food-ordering services and GPS-enabled walking directions between rides. They also wear swipeable wristbands that contain tickets, FastPasses, and payment information. The secret to the successful integration of technology is that it must add to the convenience, ease, and magic of the visit.

How to Achieve These Results in Other Businesses/ Industries

To achieve Disney-type results in other businesses, you need to truly put the customer at the center of everything you do. You have to understand the pain points, the needs, and the motivations of your customers. What are the frictions that your customers are experiencing (such as queues), and how can you transform these into a way of enhancing the overall experience? How can you proactively manage them to be part of something positive for the customer?

The other thing Disney does well is considering the physical interaction as an extension of their business. Their main business is not the amusement park—it's producing and selling movies. They use the physical components—the restaurants, theme parks, and attractions—to build engagement with the story and the brand. But it must be synergistic. It can't be something random; it needs to be something that is appealing to the customer and complements the main business. The physical components allow the customer to fully immerse themselves in the Disney experience.

The final element is to consider the data and analytics that you have available. How can you use the data to anticipate the needs of your customers and predict likely scenarios, then use your playbook as a way to normalize that relationship and reaction? Once you have determined likely scenarios, you can take out your playbook and say, "In this instance, this is going to happen, and this is how we are going to deliver for our customers—by following our predetermined playbook."

Again, think of the queues. You can anticipate that lines are going to happen. Rather than just managing the queues, how do you transform them into something enjoyable for the customer and good for the business? Into a valued part of the overall experience?

One other thought is the importance of a brand. Your brand can become the umbrella for everything that you're doing. Disney has been super intelligent by not trying to impose the Disney brand on everything they own—think Marvel/*Star Wars*—but everyone knows they belong to Disney and therefore knows what to expect from their experience. It's how Disney does things.

By creating different assets, you can set the benchmark for what customers expect but can then tailor the experience and messages to a different audience. In that respect, Disney is able to create value propositions for its different customer segments while still delivering the expected experience synonymous with the Disney ecosystem.

Questions to Ask:

1. What friction points for your customers could be transformed into part of the immersive experience?
2. How can you use data and analytics to anticipate the needs of your customers and turn this into a playbook to deliver an exceptional experience?
3. What is your overall brand umbrella—how you do things 'round here—and how can this be used to create value propositions for each customer segment?

IKEA

To create a better everyday life for the many people.

Industry	Retail—home furnishings
Overview	IKEA is an international company selling ready-to-assemble or "flat-pack" furniture and home-furnishing products. It was founded in 1943 with a vision to provide "a wide range of well-designed, functional products at prices so low that as many people as possible will be able to afford them." In 1956, it introduced "flat-packing," which reduced transportation, assembly, and inventory costs. This effectively turned customers into a free workforce that took over part of the traditional furniture manufacturing value chain. IKEA's ability to leverage the work done by its customers has enabled it to grow to 433 stores in forty-nine global markets with 957 million customers delivering a global revenue of 41.3 billion euros in 2019.

What Ikea Did Differently

In order to live up to their vision of creating "a better everyday life for the many people," IKEA believes it has to create meaning in each step of the process. Of course, this requires putting people first. To better understand how to make a difference, it is committed to listening to people's needs and dreams and working collaboratively with customers, partners, and coworkers to continue adding value to everyday lives. From start to finish, IKEA's value chain involves learning from its customers and coworkers in a circular process to "listen and learn; design and create; manufacture and improve; package and distribute; inspire and sell."

Although recognized worldwide for flat-pack furniture, IKEA didn't actually invent the concept. What it did do was bring it to the mainstream. Creating what's known as the "IKEA effect," the company leveraged the value customers place on something they have assembled themselves and the perception that, as a result, they have attained greater value for their money.

In addition, store design played a big part in its success. Each IKEA location is set up in a circular format with a one-way system. Since customers can't see what's coming next, this drives the fear that they'll miss something they need if they don't continue to the end. At the same time, the extra effort required to go back for something means that customers are more likely to immediately pick up what they see and like. Both these psychological hacks are designed to maximize customer spending.

Finally, IKEA took the idea of delivering an experience and incorporated restaurants into its stores, making it into a destination—a day out for the family. The more time customers spend in the store, the more likely they are to consume different products and the more likely it is they will buy things they had not actually intended to purchase.

IKEA then evolved the pick-and-collect format centered around a warehouse in the middle of a city where you can order, buy, and collect selected products. This evolution continued into smaller versions of IKEA stores where you can purchase bed-sheets, kitchen utensils, and other accessories, meaning it is now able to compete in categories other than furniture, such as food storage and smaller home furnishings.

This is a great example of IKEA's use of design as well as its complete understanding of the needs of its customers and how to evolve its value proposition to cater to them. If a customer lives in the middle of a city and doesn't have a car, they can still shop at IKEA and benefit from the brand's quality and value.

Ikea in the Digital Age

The unique, well-designed stores and low-cost, flat-pack furniture served IKEA well and contributed to it becoming a big player in the pre-internet furniture retail industry. But in recent years, IKEA has had to adapt to a new digital age.

Even before the pandemic, IKEA had incorporated an online channel as part of the sales mix to reflect its customers' changing habits, lifestyles, and consumption patterns. With around 75 percent of its stores closing as a result of COVID-19, it was clear IKEA needed to find digital solutions while staying true to its values and mission.

IKEA recognized that digital transformation is so much more than technology; it transforms a business. Digital technologies are a way of working, making decisions, and managing an organization, but in order to be successful, they needs to be embedded in every aspect of the company. Accordingly, IKEA recognized the need to explore potential new offers for customers, identify new ways to bring the offers to them, and investigate new ways to operate the business. The DNA of IKEA didn't change, but by adding data, increasing speed, and using analytics, the company was reinvented, or transformed, for the future.

This transformation led to the concept of human-centric technology, putting people first in all data-driven processes. IKEA is committed to providing customers with the control to make decisions about their data and thus ensured its app allows customers to edit their data at any given time. This ability to change and personalize their feed and get access to their data settings has led to the actual data captured being more relevant to their needs. Now, there is more trust and therefore more engagement.

The next step was to create a seamless, consistent customer experience by revamping customer interactions both digitally and in store and connecting them. Now, a customer might start planning their kitchen at home on ikea.com, then go into the store or connect at a remote customer meeting point. Once in store, the customer can use the "shop and go" feature of the IKEA app to scan and pay for items and skip the checkout queue.

New technologies being tested in store include virtual reality and AI. The former allows customers to visualize how a piece of furniture might fit in a room, while the latter goes one step further by letting customers scan their whole home, one room at a time. This scan is then turned into a 3D model in which the customer can try out the IKEA product range from any location. Plus, design suggestions can be made on how to furnish a room depending on the customer's budget. The IKEA 3D model library now has over thirty-three thousand models, as well as libraries for textures, materials, and props.

Technology is also being put to good use as part of the company's sustainability goals. The improvements in digital product information allow IKEA to follow the goods, trace the provenance of materials, monitor their usage, and accept the goods back for recycling. By digitally equipping customers through the app, IKEA can see this information as well as organize the return of items, enabling customers to sell back products for recycling. For this to be effective, the company needs to understand each component of the item in order to reuse materials or resell items in the stores at a cheaper price. This is facilitated by technology.

Today, 80 percent of all IKEA customer journeys start online, highlighting the importance of digital technologies in building relationships with both new and existing customers. It is up to the customers to decide which touchpoints and channels are most suitable to their needs, and this requires companies to consider new possibilities for the physical-digital channel interactions to create magical customer experiences.

The key to IKEA's successful scaling of digital initiatives is that it approaches the challenge/opportunity as an iterative process. It's about testing, building, learning, getting feedback, and analyzing data, then scaling what works and learning from what doesn't.

How to Achieve These Results in Other Businesses/ Industries

One of the things IKEA does particularly well is that it adapts to the needs of the customer. If the customer is looking for an experience, they are not going to go to the website—they are going to spend the day in store browsing through options and mixing and matching products. However, if the customer is simply looking to make a transaction, they can go to the website and pick the product they want. Then, the system will guide them to other related products they might be interested in.

Unlike Amazon, which has such a broad range of products that it's very difficult to make suitable suggestions, IKEA's e-commerce has a great setup of associated families of products. So if you're buying a bed, the IKEA system will suggest a mattress, pillows, bed sheets, candles, and so on. This allows the company to capitalize on impulse buying.

One of the problems supermarkets faced when moving online was that they lost the ability to generate additional sales through "at checkout" promotions. In fact, IKEA has mastered this so well that it is getting much better returns digitally than in store from impulse buys. As soon as you select a product, the system generates related families of products that you might be interested in purchasing. Just one click, and you've now bought not only what you were looking for but also three or four related products that you didn't know you needed.

The other thing IKEA does exceptionally well is maintain a commitment to permanent iteration and the evolution of the value proposition. It understands that the interaction with the customer has to be dynamic both in store and online. By constantly evolving the concept of a family of products, it can use data to track buying behavior, identify successful product associations, and change unsuccessful ones.

Questions to Ask:

1. How adaptable is your business to differing customer needs?
2. Is there a clear differentiation between the interaction delivered to customers wanting an experience and those simply wanting a transaction?
3. How committed are you to permanent iteration and the evolution of your value proposition, and where can you make better use of the data you collect?
4. Have you created associations between families of products/services to drive impulse buys?

RED BULL

Red Bull gives you wings.

Industry Retail—energy drink

Overview Red Bull first came to the market in 1987, a time when energy drinks didn't exist, and many doubters felt there was no demand for this type of drink. In fact, Red Bull created the market, and thirty years later, it still holds 43 percent of the fifty-three-billion-dollar market as the top-selling energy drink. In 2020, it sold 7.9 million cans across 171 countries worldwide.

What Red Bull Did Differently

At the time Red Bull was introduced to the market, traditional advertising was expensive. So it took a different approach and went straight to its target audience, eighteen- to thirty-five-year-olds, and provided free samples where they liked to hang out: at college parties, libraries, coffee shops, and bars. It put their product right into the consumers' hands, thus generating word-of-mouth advertising.

Essentially, Red Bull's strategy was to go wherever its audience was, whether that meant sponsoring music festivals or creating top-level culture content online. In effect, it became a media company that happened to sell an energy drink rather than the other way around. Selling the product came second to creating content and experiences that people would be interested in, even if they weren't interested in energy drinks.

Red Bull's slogan, "Red Bull gives you wings," focuses on the core idea that its product gives you the energy you need to do whatever you want. This underpins everything it does, giving wings to people and ideas.

Red Bull produces and records some of the most extreme, action-packed, high-flying sports, activities, and stunts ever seen. Think Felix Baumgartner launching himself into the stratosphere. This type of content keeps the audience engaged and on the edge of their seats to see if what is planned can actually be pulled off.

This is what Red Bull is all about—inspiring people to attempt the extreme with the suggestion, "What will it give you the energy and courage to do?"

Red Bull publishes a massive amount of material that doesn't even mention its product on its website—because it doesn't need to focus on its product to engage its audience. That's the clever part of Red Bull's strategy: It focuses solely on the enjoyment of its audience, not selling its product.

Red Bull's sponsorship of events and published content covers topics that interest people, like extreme sports, concerts, and music festivals. But the result is that the people who attend these events or consume the content make associations with the product that give them the energy to engage more and for longer.

Early on, Red Bull understood that in order to communicate its product, it needed to create an experience. So, it doesn't share the product's qualities, features, or formula; instead, it fully embraces the experience component. By associating the brand with edgy sports, extreme athletes, and "cool" events, consumers engage with the experience of pushing the limits, achieving the remarkable, and daring to think about and do things others wouldn't. In short, Red Bull gives them the ability to face their own challenges, achieve their aspirations, and experience life more.

How to Achieve These Results in Other Businesses/ Industries

To follow the Red Bull approach, you need to change your perspective and put your product second to the content and value you give to your customers. Focus on activities that your audience participates in while consuming your product or service. Meet your audience where they are by sponsoring events, creating opportunities to interact, and providing content online where your audience already browses rather than expecting them to come to you.

Identify the underlying value or core idea that your product gives the consumer. How does it benefit their life? What experience will the product generate? You can do this by creating regular digital content on topics that interest your target audience. Curate social media content that does not actively promote your products but that intersects your product's purpose, your brand, and your audience's interests. Produce regular updates full of cool, useful, and inspirational content that is of interest to your target audience. To succeed at content marketing in the same vein as Red Bull, you need to put your consumers' interests and experiences first.

Questions to Ask:

1. Who is your target audience?
2. Where does your target audience "hang out" both in person and online?
3. What is the experience your product/service is supposed to generate, and how does it benefit the customer's life?
4. What content is of interest or is engaging to your audience, and how does that intersect with your offering?

VITALITY

Get rewarded for better living today, so you can live a better life tomorrow.

Industry	Health/life insurance—selling health and life insurance plans to both businesses and consumers.
Overview	Vitality was the first insurance company to reward people for healthy living. Their concept is centered around the interventions they can make as an insurer that will inspire behavioral change (for the better) among their members. It's an incentive-based model that rewards members for making healthy choices through a range of partners and benefits.

What Drove the Need for Change?

Vitality is owned by Discovery Holdings, a leading global insurer with over 4.4 million clients. Based out of South Africa, Discovery, along with many other insurance companies, attained significant success using large-scale telemarketing campaigns to convert prospects to clients.

However, they started experiencing pressure from internet aggregators that came into the market, collected consumers' information, compared different insurance offers based on this data, and made recommendations. Initially, this was good for the insurance companies, as the aggregators were a great source of lead generation. They did all the data collection, suggested options for insurance based on that data, and then passed the lead on to the insurance company.

Over time, the percentage of leads being generated by these aggregators grew and started to have an impact on the traditional insurance company's business model. They found they could reduce their operating costs by lowering the number of salespeople involved in lead generation and rely more heavily on the leads provided by the comparison websites.

However, the aggregators also realized that they could evolve their business model. Essentially, instead of relying on the insurer to provide a general risk profile for a person between certain ages and calculating the premium from there, the aggregators wanted to use the data they held on individual customers to further personalize the risk profile to get them the best quote possible.

The bigger insurance companies declined to integrate further with the comparison websites, so the aggregators approached the smaller insurers. By offering to grow their quota and market share in return for integration with their risk profile generating systems, the aggregators became insurance brokers in their own right.

This was good for their business but also good for the customer. Customers were subscribing to the comparison websites, inputting their data in one place, and getting recommendations not only for health and life insurance but also for any other insurance requirements—home, car, and travel. Comparison websites were taking all the data, and the big traditional insurance companies were losing out. This is what drove the need to change and inspired their evolution.

Discovery realized it was time to reinvent their relationship with the customer. Insurance, particularly life insurance, is difficult due to the lack of public appetite for something that you have to pay for every month but get nothing back in return (hopefully!) On top of that, when you do need to claim it, it is often a long, drawn-out, and stressful process—not the best basis for a positive customer and supplier relationship.

How Did They Successfully Transform Their Business?

The initial step in their evolution was to understand the end user and put them at the center of the value proposition. What were their problems, their choices, their frictions?

The first insight was that insurance is generally offered in bulk with a broad risk profile not adjusted to the individual's circumstance or lifestyle. If you were between the ages of thirty and forty and had never smoked, you were quoted the same premium irrespective of your weight, levels of physical activity, or diet. The solution: How about rewarding people for the choices they make to adopt a healthier lifestyle?

With that, Vitality was born. The company started using technology-based incentives to drive healthier lifestyles by developing a healthier living program. If you worked at achieving ten thousand steps a day (tracked using your Apple watch or the downloadable app), you received a discount on your premium.

The idea is that if you're healthier, then you're less likely to make a claim; therefore, your risk profile diminishes, and so should your premium. Now, your premium is aligned with your behavior. The more steps you take to make healthier choices, the more rewards you earn.

By partnering with a range of companies, Vitality is able to offer various benefits, including discounts on sports shoes, spa packages, gym memberships, and health checks. Now, it's no longer an insurance provider—it's a lifestyle company that is partnering with its customers to help them become even healthier.

Remember one of the ingredients in our business transformation cocktail described in chapter four? You should be doing more than just business. Vitality is doing more than simply selling insurance—it is helping its members change their lifestyle and improve their health. In fact, Vitality data shows that those members who fully engage with making healthier lifestyle choices benefit on average from a one-and-a-half-year improvement in life expectancy.

How to Achieve These Results in Other Businesses/ Industries

To achieve these results in other businesses/industries, you really need to get into the shoes of your customer and understand the frictions—the problems—they experience with your company, the market, or the industry. Most leaders assume that the frictions are there but that they can't do anything about them—it's just part of the equation. They often think, *Insurance is just painful and one sided.*

But in come the disruptors doing something completely different, and now they've changed the customers' expectations. Customers no longer want to have to input their data over and over again in each insurance company's system.

As long as the status quo continues, companies can continue to treat their customers the way they've always been and now expect to be treated. That's just the way it is. But the moment the disruptors—in this case, the aggregators—turn up and say they're going to fix all this inefficiency and all these frictions, you have to change your approach.

You have to really understand that the value is not in providing the insurance, which is the less attractive part for the end user. It's in the fact that the insurance company, using the data it holds, can start a conversation on a different level. It's about taking something that your customer needs to have—that they don't really want to engage with and that's just painful because they have to pay for it—and turning it into something that your customer wants to talk about and can actually see a benefit from.

By evolving your approach from focusing on transactions to becoming a platform—in Vitality's case, building a network of gyms—you can incentivize your partners to recommend your products/services as well as reward your customers every time they use one of your partners. Gyms that partner with Vitality get rewarded for recommending Vitality's insurance, Vitality gets access to further data about their members' behavior and healthy habits, and members of Vitality's healthier living program receive rewards every time they use the gym. Win-win-win. Now, you're bigger than your original purpose. You're doing more than just business!

Questions to Ask:

1. What was the original purpose of your business?
2. What problem are you trying to solve?
3. What is your purpose that goes beyond making money and supports a cause that benefits mankind?
4. How can you transform your customers' experience?

CONCLUSION

As this book winds to a close and our journey through the world of digital transformation comes to an end, I hope you have gained the critical knowledge you need to leverage design as the route to digital transformation in your organization. In the pages of this book, you've not only learned how to leverage design to effect business transformation, but you've also examined many success stories of digital transformation through an emphasis on design. It is my fervent hope that you've seen how those lessons can (and should) be applied in your organization.

Remember, design is dynamic, it's evolutionary, and it focuses less on the specific challenges of the current moment and more on whether you've created the design infrastructure to pivot toward an effective, efficient response. Simply put, design is a strategic business asset that helps organizations innovate and grow. It's gone from being merely concerned with aesthetics to being a measure of user centricity and an engine for creating meaningful experiences and improved business performance.

If you take away one message from this book, it should be that a successful future requires businesses to engage in the process of continuous reinvention. With that in mind, it's crucial that you aim to embrace the challenges and opportunities provided by disruptors as well as develop the ability to build unique relationships both inside and outside your enterprise. Ultimately, partnership and value proposition extensions should be considered the norm.

All in all, design is in everything, and it's crucial to your business's financial performance. It creates experiences that drive behavior and provides an opportunity for digital-based evolution.

Above all, design is about intention—acting with purpose. That is my challenge to you: How will you intentionally use design to transform your organization?

YOUR TRANSFORMATION TOOLKIT—THE PATH TO DIGITAL [R]EVOLUTION

Step 1—Know Yourself

- Where are you today?
- Are you in a growing phase?
- Are you being challenged?
- Is your industry being disrupted?
- How is the regulatory environment?
- What has been the main source of your company's revenue?
- What's the most important asset you have?
- What data are you currently collecting?
- How are you using this data?
- Is all the data in one place (customer persona/profile)?
- Is there data that is not currently being utilized?
- What are your core values?
- Are you doing more than just business? Do you have a purpose?
- What do your KPIs focus on?

Step 2—Detach Yourself

- What might you have to be prepared to abandon in order to evolve?
- What has previously made you successful but now may be holding you back?

Step 3—Creating Experiences

- How does your customer experience the journey, product, process, and interaction with your business?
- How can you best engage with your customers?
- How can you best help, advise, and support your customers?
- What interactions need to remain in the physical world, and how can you add more value to these interactions?
- How are you going to complement the physical part with the digital part?
- What are you going to do digitally while incorporating interaction with human beings, and what are you going to automate?
- Examine your touchpoints with the customer. How does this information allow you to give your customer a better experience?

Step 4—Taking Care of the Relationship

- How can you use the information you already hold about your customers/collaborators to better understand who they are and what they care about?
- How do you put your customers'/collaborators' problems, concerns, and issues at the center of your value

proposition? How does this combine with your business objectives, regulatory landscape, and industry situation to determine the value proposition that makes it to market?

- Are you co-creating with your customers/collaborators based on a business opportunity that lies in the market or in your assets?
- How can you reimagine the relationship you have with your customer as one powered and boosted by digital technology?
- By looking at the data you already hold, can you understand the life events taking place for your customers and turn this insight into an action to create a better relationship with them?

Step 5—Your Backpack of Solutions

- Reevaluate your business model.
    - o How do you turn your business model from one that sells a product or service (e.g., health insurance) to one that allows your customer to experience a better life (e.g., being healthier)?
- Define your playbook experience.
    - o The moment you develop your playbook, you start developing KPIs to track that experience.
- Generate data, actionable insights, and loyalty.
    - o The important point here is that you need to be able to profile your customer. That way, you can offer personalized experiences to your target audiences by understanding who they are and how they are connected to your value proposition.

- Explore platforms.
  - o Becoming a platform business requires you to reinterpret your assets.
  - o How can you make your assets more scalable?
- Creating the WOW factor!
  - o How are you going to surprise and delight priority customers, whether individuals or target groups?

Sneak Peek of *Disruption, Designed*

It's important to note that this book is part of a two-book series focused on the evolution of the modern enterprise driven by design and powered by technology and data.

In the second book, *Disruption, Designed*, we discuss how design-driven strategies can be used to create digital disruption and generate new business models, customer experiences, and market platforms. We will delve into the fundamentals of disruption—its basic components, enablers, failures, and key success factors. We will examine case studies of digital disruption executed, and finally, I will share with you the recipe that I have been using with dozens of clients around the world to create disruption.

> "For an incumbent, disruption is not about innovation. It's about reinterpreting user needs and company assets to create a new value proposition that will deliver something faster, cheaper, and with a superior customer experience, all enabled by technology and data."
>
> —J.J. de la Torre

BIBLIOGRAPHY

Allen, James, Frederick F. Reichheld, Barney Hamilton, and Rob Markey. "Closing the delivery gap." Bain & Company. 2005. https://media.bain.com/bainweb/PDFs/cms/hotTopics/closingdeliverygap.pdf.

Amarsy, Nabila. "Disney's business model: a scalable dream factory." Strategyzer. March 17, 2015. https://www.strategyzer.com/library/disneys-business-model-a-scalable-dream-factory.

Barbour, Hilton. "Culture & Digital Transformation: building a culture of transformation at Ikea." The Digital Transformation People. June 23, 2020. https://www.thedigitaltransformationpeople.com/channels/people-and-change/culture-digital-transformation-building-a-culture-of-transformation-at-ikea/.

Beck, Elias. "Invention of the automobile (Model T)." History Crunch. Last updated March 25, 2022. https://www.historycrunch.com/invention-of-the-automobile-model-t.html#/.

Becker, John. "20 Value Proposition Examples that Every Marketer Can Learn From in 2024." iMPACT. Last updated January 18, 2024. https://www.impactplus.com/blog/value-proposition-examples.

Bianchini, R. "Apple iPhone's design – from the 1st generation to the iPhone 12." 2021. https://www.inexhibit.com/case-studies/apple-iphone-history-of-a-design-revolution/

Bonnet, Didier and Michael R. Wade. "Unpacking the digital transformation at Ikea." IMD. February 15, 2022. https://iby.imd.org/innovation/unpacking-the-digital-transformation-at-ikea/.

Boutetière, Hortense de la, Alberto Montagner, and Angelika Reich. "Unlocking success in digital transformations." McKinsey & Company. October 29, 2018. https://www.mckinsey.com/business-functions/people-and-organizational-performance/our-insights/unlocking-success-in-digital-transformations.

Clement, Matt. "Warby Parker Becomes Massive Through Understanding the Market." Nxtbook Media. June 19, 2019. https://www.nxtbookmedia.com/blog/warby-parker/.

CM Commerce Team. "The Ultimate List of Omnichannel Marketing Examples and Statistics." CM Commerce. July 31, 2020. https://cm-commerce.com/academy/ultimate-list-of-omnichannel-marketing-examples-statistics/.

"Content Marketing Success: Two Case Studies." SocialMediaToday. January 27, 2015. https://www.socialmediatoday.com/content/content-marketing-success-two-case-studies.

Cortes, Luis Perez and Kevin Close. "Designing Experience: A Case Study of Disneyland's Lines." Talking About Design. January 8, 2020. https://talkingaboutdesign.com/designing-experience-a-case-study-of-disneylands-lines/.

"Customer Archetypes and Buyer Personas: A fundamental step for your startup or software business." Cobuild Lab. https://www.cobuildlab.com/blog/buyer-persona-and-customer-archetype-for-software-business/.

Ehrlich, Oliver, Harald Fanderl, and Christian Habrich. "Mastering the digital advantage in transforming customer experience." McKinsey & Company. May 3, 2017. https://www.mckinsey.com/capabilities/operations/our-insights/mastering-the-digital-advantage-in-transforming-customer-experience.

Elmansky, Rafiq. "Design Thinking Case Study: Innovation at Apple." Designorate. April 7, 2016. https://www.designorate.com/design-thinking-case-study-innovation-at-apple/.

"Energy Drink Market Trends, Growth and Growth Rate in 2022." Green Seed. May 24, 2021. https://greenseedgroup.com/energy-drink-market-trends-growth-and-growth-rate-in-2022/#:~:text=find%20out%20below.-,How%20much%20market%20share%20does%20Red%20Bull%20have%3F,share%20of%20the%20global%20market.

"Evolution of Microsoft Word." Version Museum. https://www.versionmuseum.com/history-of/microsoft-word.

Faller, Patrick. "Putting Personas to Work in UX Design: What They Are and Why They're Important." Adobe. December 17, 2019. https://xd.adobe.com/ideas/process/user-research/putting-personas-to-work-in-ux-design/.

"Ford Heritage: The Ford Motor Company Story." Ford. https://www.ford.co.uk/experience-ford/history-and-heritage.

Forrester. "The Total Economic Impact of IBM's Design Thinking Practice." IBM. February 2018. https://www.ibm.com/design/thinking/static/Enterprise-Design-Thinking-Report-8ab1e9e1622899654844a5fe1d760ed5.pdf.

Gabay, Ron. "Design-led innovation: lessons from the scientific revolution." *Interactions* 27, no. 5 (2020). https://doi.org/10.1145/3418604.

García, Tomás Ferrari. "Design and the Fourth Industrial Revolution. Dangers and opportunities for a mutating discipline." *The Design Journal* 20, no. 1 (2017). https://doi.org/10.1080/14606925.2017.1352774.

Goran, Julie, Laura LaBerge, and Ramesh Srinivasan. "Culture for a digital age." McKinsey & Company. July 20, 2017. https://www.mckinsey.com/capabilities/mckinsey-digital/our-insights/culture-for-a-digital-age#/.

Grenier, Louis. "How to create a user persona in 3 steps (with a free template)." *Hotjar* (blog). Last updated July 29, 2024. https://www.hotjar.com/blog/user-personas/.

"How Henry Ford's engineering genius drove an industrial revolution." Autodesk. August 10, 2021. https://redshift.autodesk.com/videos/henry-fords-manufacturing-innovations.

Hoyer, Wayne D., Mirja Kroschke, Bernd Schmitt, Karsten Kraume, Venkatesh Shankar. "Transforming the Customer Experience through New Technologies." *Journal of Interactive Marketing* 51, no. 1 (2020). https://doi.org/10.1016/j.intmar.2020.04.001.

"Ikea's DesignOps revolution." *NODE* Podcast. February 9, 2021. https://www.digitalbulletin.com/CaseStudies/Technology/2020/December/ikea/ikeas-designops-revolution/.

"Is it true that about 4,000 features of Microsoft Excel are never used?" Quora. https://www.quora.com/Is-it-true-that-about-4-000-features-of-Microsoft-Excel-are-never-used.

Jacquemont, David, Dana Maor, and Angelika Reich. "Losing from day one: Why even successful transformations fall short." McKinsey & Company. December 7, 2021. https://www.mckinsey.com/business-functions/people-and-organizational-performance/our-insights/successful-transformations.

Johnston, Matthew. "How Disney Makes Money: Entertainment, Sports, and Experiences." Investopedia. Last updated September 23, 2024. https://www.investopedia.com/how-disney-makes-money-4799164.

Khan, Ayan. "Red Bull Marketing Strategy: The Case Study." *Mix with Marketing* (blog). February 20, 2024. https://mixwithmarketing.com/2022/02/red-bull-marketing-strategy-the-case-study/.

Kristina. "9 Best Value Proposition Examples + How to Create One." *sixads* (blog). March 31, 2021. https://sixads.net/blog/value-proposition-examples/.

Krom, Ipek. "Experiential Marketing and Online Consumer Engagement That Carry Your Brand to the Future: Legoland Case." In *New Trends in Management Studies* edited by Özer Yilmaz, 149-163. Peter Lang, 2021. https://www.researchgate.net/publication/348662592.

Lemon, Katherine N. and Peter C. Verhoef, P.C. "Understanding Customer Experience Throughout the Customer Journey." *Journal of Marketing* 80 (2016): 69-96. https://phavi.umcs.pl/at/attachments/2017/0422/113134-2016-customer-journej-verhoef.pdf.

Libai, Barak, Ruth Bolton, Marnix S. Bügel, Ko de Ruyter, Oliver Götz, Hans Risselada, and Andrew T. Stephen. "Customer-to-Customer Interactions: Broadening the Scope of Word of Mouth Research." *Journal of Service Research* 13, no. 3 (2010). https://doi.org/10.1177/1094670510375600.

Long, Michael. "Why Red Bull Media House Is the 'King of Content'." SportsPro. March 22, 2019. https://www.sportspromedia.com/from-the-magazine/red-bull-media-house-video-content-gerrit-meier-interview/.

Meyer, Chris and Andre Schwager. "Understanding Customer Experience." *Harvard Business Review.* February 2007. https://hbr.org/2007/02/understanding-customer-experience.

Moore, Carol. "The new heart of your brand: Transforming your business through customer experience." *Design Management Review* 13, (2002): 39-48. https://doi.org/10.1111/j.1948-7169.2002.tb00297.x.

Morgan, Blake. "5 Lessons From Disney's Magical Customer Experience." *Forbes.* Last updated December 10, 2021. https://www.forbes.com/sites/blakemorgan/2020/01/23/5-lessons-from-disneys-magical-customer-experience/?sh=3fc4a3557555.

Pine, Joseph P. II and Gilmore, James H. "The experience economy: past, present and future." In *Handbook on the Experience Economy,* edited by Jon Sundbo and Flemming Sørensen, 269. Edward Elgar Publishing, 2013. https://www.researchgate.net/publication/260917972_The_experience_economy_past_present_and_future.

Rae, Jeneanne. "What Is the Real Value of Design?" *Design Management Review* 24, (2013): 30-37. https://www.dmi.org/page/13244RAE30.

Roberts, Tessa. "What Is Omnichannel Commerce? The Benefits and Ways to Build an Omnichannel Strategy for Retail."

Bloomreach (blog). Last updated August 28, 2024. https://www.bloomreach.com/en/blog/2019/07/omnichannel-commerce-for-business.html.

Rosoff, Matt. "Why is tech getting cheaper?" World Economic Forum. October 16, 2015. https://www.weforum.org/agenda/2015/10/why-is-tech-getting-cheaper/.

Saracco, Roberto. "A never ending decrease of technology cost." *IEEE Future Directions* (blog). October 18, 2017. https://cmte.ieee.org/futuredirections/2017/10/18/a-never-ending-decrease-of-technology-cost/.

Shastri, Aditya. "IKEA's Business Model: Global Furniture Analysis." Indian Institute of Digital Education. Last updated July 24, 2024. https://iide.co/case-studies/business-model-of-ikea/.

Sheppard, Benedict, Hugo Sarrazin, Garen Kouyoumjian, and Fabricio Dore. "The business value of design." *McKinsey Quarterly.* October 25, 2018. https://www.mckinsey.com/business-functions/mckinsey-design/our-insights/the-business-value-of-design.

Shewan, Dan. "7 of the Best Value Proposition Examples We've Ever Seen." *Wordstream* (blog). Last updated October 23, 2024. https://www.wordstream.com/blog/ws/2016/04/27/value-proposition-examples.

Sorrentino, Dominick. "Customer Archetype: What Is It and How Do You Build One?" Brafton. August 4, 2023. https://www.brafton.com/blog/strategy/customer-archetype/.

Stackpole, Thomas. "Inside Ikea's Digital Transformation." *Harvard Business Review.* June 4, 2021. https:///hbr.org/2021/06/inside-ikeas-digital-transformation.

Stone, Merlin, Eleni Aravopoulou, Gherardo Girardi, Paul Laughlin, Ryan Stott, Emanuela Todeva, and Luisa Weinzierl. "How platforms are transforming customer information management." *The Bottom Line* 30, no. 3 (2017). https://doi.org/10.1108/BL-08-2017-0024.

Tabrizi, Behnam, Ed Lam, Kirk Gerard, and Vernon Irvin. "Digital Transformation Is Not About Technology." *Harvard Business Review.* March 13, 2019. https://hbr.org/2019/03/digital-transformation-is-not-about-technology.

Tawakley, Hardeep. "Case study: What does the future of health insurance really look like?" *Cover* Magazine. August 24, 2021. https://www.covermagazine.co.uk/sponsored/4035642/case-study-future-health-insurance-look.

Toader, Georgian. "Omnichannel vs Multichannel What's the Difference?" NobelBiz. Last updated March 20, 2023. https://nobelbiz.com/omnichannel-vs-multichannel/.

Turner, Rich. "Windows Command-Line: The Evolution of the Windows Command-Line." Microsoft. June 27, 2018. https://devblogs.microsoft.com/commandline/windows-command-line-the-evolution-of-the-windows-command-line/.

Venkatesh, Ashreya, Kristin Lee Wood, and Arlindo Silva. "Measuring Design In Business and Government—A Framework to Measure Design Impact." In *Design for Tomorrow—Volume 2: Proceedings of ICoRD 2021,* edited by Amaresh Chakrabarti, Ravi Poovaiah, Prasad Bokil, and Vivek Kant. Springer, 2021.

Weiss, Juliette. "A Brief History of Microsoft Design." Medium. April 4, 2017. https://medium.com/microsoft-design/a-brief-history-of-design-8641bd186e00.

Westcott, Michael, Steve Sato, Deb Mrazek, Rob Wallace, Surya Vanka, Carole Bilson, and Dianne Hardin. "The DMI Design Value Scorecard: A New Design Measurement and Management Model." *Design Management Review*. 2013. https://www.dmi.org/store/viewproduct.aspx?id=2481474.

Wilder, Jake. "How Disney Does Customer Experiences Better Than Anyone." Medium. November 22, 2019. https://marker.medium.com/how-to-deliver-an-amazing-customer-experience-50d9c3dbcb67.

Wirtz, Jochen. *Crafting the Service Environment.* World Scientific, 2017.

Zacher, Chris. "How to Build Customer Archetypes and Buyer Personas." Intergrowth. Last updated October 2, 2023. https://inter-growth.co/content-marketing/customer-archetypes/.

ABOUT THE AUTHOR – J.J. DE LA TORRE

A world reference in digital businesses, disruption, and digital transformation, Juan Jose (J.J.) is an expert in the areas of strategy, innovation, and all things digital. He has been recognized as one of the world's top eighteen digital transformation leaders and a top five digital marketing influencer.

A true digital hero and design evangelist, J.J. is a senior executive with almost two decades of experience across America, Europe, Asia, Africa, and the Middle East. J.J.'s profile combines a unique blend of corporate, consulting, and entrepreneurial experience.

Following his return to his home country, Chile, after twenty years of a successful international career, J.J. joined Virtus Partners as a senior partner. At Virtus, J.J. led the organization's digital endeavors, which turned into the establishment of Raven, a unique consulting boutique solely focused on business disruption and acceleration. As Raven's CEO, J.J. pools strategy, design, technology, and analytics to help clients across industries embrace digital enablers and technologies to create business disruption and accelerate their growth while reinventing and reimagining their processes, operations, and employee engagement.

A real digital business disruptor and transformation leader, J.J. showcases his leadership through various platforms, including *Entrepreneur*, *VICE*, *Fast Company*, and *The Huffington Post*, and holds a Twitter/X audience that exceeds thirty thousand followers. J.J. has delivered more than two hundred keynotes while gaining international recognition in global media, including *Forbes, Financial Times, Wall Street Journal*, and Bill & Melinda Gates Foundation, among others. He has been an advisor to the United Nations, the Organisation for Economic Co-operation and Development, and the Banco Interamericano de Desarrollo (BID) on mobility, innovation, and entrepreneurship subjects and has largely authored in the areas of digital, innovation, and entrepreneurship.

An angel investor for fourteen start-ups, a mentor for more than 150 companies, and the founder of the first information and communications technology incubator in Saudi Arabia as well as the first 360 accelerator in the Middle East, J.J. has also founded and successfully traded three start-ups.

J.J. holds an MBA from INSEAD, a master's degree from La Salle, and an industrial engineering degree from Adolfo Ibanez. He has been awarded the INSEAD Eli Lilly Innovation Scholarship, the Fundación Carolina (Spanish government) Excellence Scholarship, and the Chilean Banks and Financial Institutions Associations Award.

A father of three and loving husband to wife Maria, J.J. is a former professional DJ and now music composer, a PADI diving instructor, and a mountain bike and golf aficionado. He enjoys traveling and adventure sports.